The Genesis Revelation Connection:
THE SCROLL

Anthony Lyle

authorHOUSE®

AuthorHouse™
1663 Liberty Drive
Bloomington, IN 47403
www.authorhouse.com
Phone: 1 (800) 839-8640

Published by AuthorHouse 08/31/2018

ISBN: 978-1-5462-5867-4 (sc)
ISBN: 978-1-5462-5866-7 (hc)
ISBN: 978-1-5462-5865-0 (e)

Library of Congress Control Number: 2018910457

Print information available on the last page.

Scripture taken from The Holy Bible, King James Version. Public Domain

CONTENTS

INTRODUCTION

This work does not claim to be THE absolute truth, but a guide to help those who seek to find the truth. It is Biblically based and is intended to help understand the many confusing things said about the Bible by so-called educated professionals.

CHAPTER 1

TIME

1. Dating Historical Events: Without calendars and relative dating methods, historical events have no relative connections and no relevance. A business appointment between two or more people only has culpability if all parties have a reliable and similar basis of time allowing them to all appear at the same place at the same time.

Ancient historical events have the same need of a reliable dating method, i.e. calendars. As important as calendars are to history books, it is amazing that more historians don't spend more time in discussing the many varieties of calendars throughout history. In our western history books, it is assumed the Julian/Gregorian calendar is the basis for dating historical events. Events that are dated before 44 B.C. are based on the *proleptic* Julian calendar or the "pretend" calendar, since the calendar didn't exist at the time of the event.

2. Measurement of Time: The standard physical aspects of time (day, year, or season) have been known to every society. Each society has measured these aspects and divided them or grouped them by different methods. The Western Calendar (Julian or Gregorian) is not the same calendar as the Hebrew or the Islamic Calendar. Some calendars are lunar based, some solar based, some empirical (static without regard to the motions of the earth), and or a combination of the three. The ancient Aztecs even had a Venus based calendar.

Matching the different calendars to achieve accurate historical dates based on the different calendars can be tricky. One of the best ways to do this is to count days, but even this allows some degree of error in matching a date from an ancient Babylonian Calendar to a modern Gregorian calendar date. There are mainly 3 known systems for counting days, and all three are very similar, usually with different "Epochs" or starting dates.

2a. Julian Day Count: This system is not named after the calendar system of the same name but was devised by Joseph Scaliger who named the system after his father, Julian Scaliger. By calculating known cycles of time back to a beginning point where they all converged, he decided that the starting point for counting days should be Jan 1, 4713 B.C. (This matches to Nov 24, 2712 B.C. in the Gregorian calendar). This becomes his Epoch. The Epochs for most calendars are given in Julian/Gregorian dates for Western statistics. Jan 1, 4713 B.C. became Day 1.

2b. Lillian Day Count: Pope Gregory decreed that the Julian Calendar should be corrected as astronomers of his time declared that the calendar was 11 days off from the astronomical placement of earth. The official change took place on Oct 4, 1582 A.D. The next day after the 4th was declared to be the 11th, so there was no 5th through 10th of October in this year. Since the Julian Day count proved to be successful for many reasons, it was thought that a similar system should be declared, called the Lilian Day Count. Day 1 of the Lillian Day Count is equivalent to day 2299160 J.D. This removes errors that can take place over long periods of times in many algorithms by bringing the time down more measurable lengths.

2c. Rata Dies Count: A more modern approach, created by Edward M. Reingold and Nachum Dershowitz came about because of the inaccuracy of the algorithms over long periods of times. In their system, the time periods are divided in half to decrease the algorithmic errors. They assigned Jan 1, 1 A.D. as their Day 1 (equivalent to J.D. 1721425.5). The reason for the .5 is that they decided that midnight would be a better time to start their count. The Julian Day count changes at noon each day.

2d. Dies Torah Count: This system is derived from the Biblical Epoch of Creation Day being day 1, which is estimated to be Mar 22, 3963 B.C. or 273685 J.D. or -1,447,340.5 R.D. This is the main method of counting days used in this work. It must be noted that due to the shift in the earth's motion around 715 B.C., counting days accurately after this point has many pitfalls and can't be used to accurately count the days to the end of the 7000 years of history predicted by the Bible. The Hebrew orthodox does not believe that counting days is legal and thus they refrain from doing so.

2e. Start of Day for different cultures: Our western day has traditionally started at Midnight, but that is not true with all cultures. In Israel, the start of the day is the time around 6 P.M. or the beginning of the night time, dusk. In ancient Egypt, the start of the day was around 6 A.M. or the beginning of the light of day, dawn.

The Julian Day Count system created by Scaliger, he assigned to start at Noon, which is why the J.D. counts usually include a .5 in the count (half a day). The Rata Dies count uses Midnight to match that of the western culture, as does the Lilian Day Count. The Dies Torah count uses the traditional Biblical definition of the day where the night starts each day (6 P.M.), (dusk as in the Hebrew culture).

Time of Start of each Day by a few calendars and systems: This makes a huge difference when trying to match days from one calendar to the other.

Physical Night	Day	Night	Day	Night	
J.D. 1	J.D. 2		J.D.3		
D.T. 1		D.T.2		D.T.3	
Hebrew A.M. Day 1		Day 2		Day 3	
Egyptian Day 1	Day 2		Day 3		
R.D. 1	Julian Calendar and Rata Dies 2		Day 3		Day 4

2f. Start of the Year for different cultures: Archaeological finds that define ancient calendars (i.e. Egypt, Israel, Babylon, India, and even Greece) show that all cultures around the globe started their year on the Spring Equinox. All the calendars had their day 1 on the Gregorian Date of March 21. It must be added here that ALL cultures of that time used a calendar of 360 days. Historians have declared that the ancients used a calendar in error of the cosmological system that we now know as they believe the solar system has remained unchanged for millions of years. There is a considerable amount of proof to show that our modern historians and scientists are in error, as will be shown.

The Hebrews, when they began to compile a more modern version of their history around 200 A.D. moved the beginning of the year to Tishrei 1 or around the Autumnal Equinox. Even after the cultures of the world modified their calendars to add 5 days to the year, (between 700 B.C. and 600 B.C.) they continued to use the Spring Equinox as the start of the year.

The first Julian calendar (separate from the Julian Day count) adopted by Augustus Cesar and made official in 8 A.D. originally started in March as well, with March being the 1st month. January and February months added at the last were numbered 11 and 12. Early in the history of the Roman year (Julian calendar) they moved the start of the calendar to January 1st.

The idea that the original calendar makers were in error is in itself error prone as these same ancient astronomers were able to calculate pi to 10 decimal places without a computer and it would have been impossible for them to miss the fact that their calendar was moving by 5 days each year. No adjustments of ancient calendars were ever recorded. The only changes known throughout the ancient world took place after 715 B.C. when every culture scrambled to make the changes to their calendars. Why did it take 2000 years to realize that there were 365 days per year? The ancients recorded that they had measure the revolution of the earth to an accurate 360 days per year. It was not an error. Around 715 B.C. the earth was influenced by cosmological forces to move slower around the sun by 5 days. (Note: Immanuel Velikovsky reports that the change of the earth's revolution took place in 689 B.C.).

2g. Yovel: The yovel or jubilee is a Biblically defined time reference and is super important when considering the plan of HaShem. It either refers to a 49 year period or a 50 year period, depending on the historian. For this revised reference, it is believed to be a 50 year reference of time.

> Leviticus 25: 8-22 is quoted as follows: "Count off seven Sabbaths of years–seven times seven years–so that the seven Sabbaths of years amount to a period of forty-nine years. Then have the trumpet sounded everywhere on the

tenth day of the seventh month; on the Day of Atonement sound the trumpet throughout your land. Consecrate the fiftieth year and proclaim liberty throughout the land to all its inhabitants. It shall be a jubilee for you; each one of you is to return to his family property and each to his own clan. The fiftieth year shall be a jubilee for you; do not sow and do not reap what grows of itself or harvest the untended vines. For it is a jubilee and is to be holy for you; eat only what is taken directly from the fields. In this Year of Jubilee everyone is to return to his own property. If you sell land to one of your countrymen or buy any from him, do not take advantage of each other. You are to buy from your countryman on the basis of the number of years since the Jubilee. And he is to sell to you on the basis of the number of years left for harvesting crops. When the years are many, you are to increase the price, and when the years are few, you are to decrease the price, because what he is really selling you is the number of crops. Do not take advantage of each other, but fear your God. I am HaShem your God. Follow my decrees and be careful to obey my laws, and you will live safely in the land. Then the land will yield its fruit, and you will eat your fill and live there in safety. You may ask, 'What will we eat in the seventh year if we do not plant or harvest our crops?' I will send you such a blessing in the sixth year that the land will yield enough for *three* years. While you plant during the *eighth* year, you will eat from the old crop and will continue to eat from it until the harvest of the *ninth* year comes in." (Italics mine)

Normal Planting						No Planting	Normal Planting					
1	2	3	4	5	6	Sabbath Year	1	2	3	4	5	6

Shabbath Cycle of Years

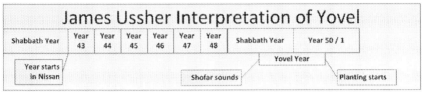

James Ussher Interpretation of Yovel

Shabbath Year	Year 43	Year 44	Year 45	Year 46	Year 47	Year 48	Shabbath Year	Year 50 / 1

Year starts in Nissan

Yovel Year

Shofar sounds

Planting starts

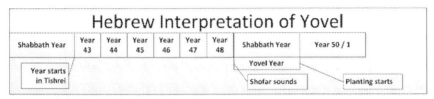

Hebrew Interpretation of Yovel

Shabbath Year	Year 43	Year 44	Year 45	Year 46	Year 47	Year 48	Shabbath Year	Year 50 / 1

Year starts in Tishrei

Yovel Year

Shofar sounds

Planting starts

Revised (Lyle) Interpretation of Yovel

Shabbath Year	Year 43	Year 44	Year 45	Year 46	Year 47	Year 48	Shabbath Year / Year 49	Second Shabbath Year / Year 50	Year 1 of New Yovel

Year starts in Nissan

Yovel Year

Shofar sounds

Planting starts

The Talmud has this to say about the Yovel: "Therefore it says, it is a Jubilee to you, the fiftieth year, [to show that] you are *to sanctify the fiftieth year, but not the fifty-first* year." The Hizkuni believes that Sefira and Shavuot are somehow reminders for the really important mitzvoth: Shemita and Yovel. Every seventh year is considered a Shemita year, meaning that land in Eretz Ysrael may not be worked and that all debts owed by Jews to other Jews are canceled. Every fiftieth year is considered Yovel ("Jubilee"), meaning that all Jewish slaves are freed and that all land which has changed hands in the years since the last Yovel now returns to the hands of its original owner. What clues the Hizkuni in to the connection between Sefira/Shavuot and Shemita/Yovel? There are several likely possibilities

The Midrash also reports on the Yovel: "...count forty-nine days, and sanctify the fiftieth, just like Yovel (Sifra 167:8)." The Ramban emphasizes it further: "the number of days from the day of waving (the Omer offering) until Yom Tov (Shavuot) is as the number of years of the Shemita until the Yovel; the reasoning for both is identical." Thus, it behooves us to clarify this connection, and then to try to assimilate this understanding into our observance of the mitzvah of Sefiras HaOmer and preparation for Shavuot

The Talmud: Rosh Hashanah 9a And the Rabbis [— what do they make of these words]? — [They say]: You are to count the fiftieth year, but you are not to count the fifty-first, to exclude the view of R. Judah, who said that the fiftieth year is reckoned both ways. We are here told that this is not so. Rashi indicates that we count seven Shemita years and then we consecrate the fiftieth year. This fiftieth year is not the first year of the next cycle. Tosafot says: 'you are to count the fiftieth year (as fiftieth to the Jubilee), but you are not to count the fiftieth year as one (to the following septennate)'

Yechezkel (Ezekiel) 40:1: In the fifth year of our exile, at the beginning of the year, on the tenth of the month, in the fourteenth year after the fall of the city–on that very day the hand of HaShem was upon me and he took me there.
According to the Talmud, this was a jubilee year, while the Release years (Shemita) and Jubilee years did not commence until the land had been divided. The calculation is then as follows: The Temple was built four hundred and eighty years after the Shemoth (Exodus), which was four hundred and forty years after their entry into Eretz Israel. The Temple stood four hundred and ten years, making a total of eight hundred and fifty years from their entry until its destruction, which is the thirty-seventh

Jubilee. Deducting fourteen years for conquest and division, as these did not count for Jubilee, we find that it was destroyed fourteen years before a Jubilee year, and therefore the fourteenth year after its destruction was a Jubilee year. (The Talmud deduces that this was a Jubilee year independently of this calculation.)

Arachin 13a According to the Midrash (Tehillim (Psalms) 90:4), "the Torah preceded the world by 2000 years." In accordance with the Torah command designating every fiftieth year to be Yovel (the jubilee year, in which farmers in Israel are forbidden to work the land), the 2000th year was the fortieth Yovel year. Thus, the first five days of creation were therefore the last five days of the fortieth Yovel year.

It is the premise here that HaShem intended for 2 different Yovel counts. The first started when Adam took possession of the land after the expulsion from the Garden of Eden. This means that *this* yovel applies to all men, as it was not limited to Israel. The second applies to Israel only and starts when Joshua leads the Israelites into Canaan to inhabit or possess the land of Israel. To the Israelites, the Yovel does not apply to Goyim as it was given to Moses as part of the law. The problem with this interpretation is that both Abraham and Jacob were both well aware of the laws given to Moses 400 years before it was given to Moses. If the law were to ONLY apply to Israelites, then Goyim could not attain salvation at all and this is outside of the Plan of HaShem.

3. **Calendars and changes:** William Whiston, "*New Theory of the Earth*", shows that the classic historians of the ancient worlds all supported the concept of a 360 day year. The "*Nidana Sutra*" of India gives the exact calculation of the calendar used in India as a 360 day calendar. The "*Arabhatiya*" of India gives the exact same calculations. Changes to the calendars in India did not come about until after 700 B.C. Now, India, like China uses two calendars, one a lunar based and one a solar based.

They have extreme algorithms to calculate their calendars based on the planets and stars, not just on the moon and the sun.

Immanuel Velikovsky, *"Worlds in Collision"*, gives evidence that Babylon and Assyria both used a 360 day calendar before 700 B.C. In Greece, Cleobulus defined a Greek calendar of 360 days. Around 600 B.C. the calendar of Greece was changed to add 5 days. In Rome, Numa had to *correct* the calendar that was being used in Rome to add 5 days to the calendar.

In Egypt, the *Canopus Decree* and the *Eber Papyrus*, of the 18th Dynasty, defined the calendar of 360 days. The *Book of Sothis*, from the Hyksos Period, gives the same calculations. The extra 5 days of the Egyptian calendar, called *Epagomenic Days*, were added after 700 B.C. and they were considered bad luck due to the circumstances of why they had to be added. The extra 5 days became the 13th month of their calendar.

The Mayans and the Chinese cultures both added 5 days to their calendars after 700 B.C. There are many archaeological documents that support these changes, leading to a definite conclusion of the year being a 360 day year before 700 B.C.

While a statement was made earlier that it is strange that historians do not discuss calendars in most history books, there have been some historians who saw some of the problems of translating from one cultural calendar to another after 700 B.C. Many algorithms were great for short periods of time, but over longer periods of time, the algorithms started to fail in their accuracy. *"Calendrical Calculations"* is a modern book that looks at calendar conversion algorithms and is responsible for the creation of the Rata Dies Day count system. They give the Epochs or starting point of many of our modern calendars of multiple cultures.

Calendar	Julian	Gregorian	J.D.	R.D.
Alexandrian	09 20, 23 BC	09 26, 23 BC	1712927	-8098
Anc. Babylon	03 23, 2241 BC	03 04, 2241 BC	902614	-818811
Anc. Egypt	03 14, 2148 BC	02 25, 2148 BC	936574	-784851
Armenian	07 11, 552 AD	07 13, 552 AD	1922868	201443
Armenian, Lit	08 11, 1084 AD			
Astronomical	12 19, 1999 AD	01 01 2000 AD	2451545	730121
Aztec	08 13, 1521 AD	08 22, 1521 AD	2276827	555403
Baha'i	03 11, 1844 AD	03 21, 1844 AD	2394710	673222
Celtic				
Chinese	03 08, 2637 BC	02 15, 2636 BC	758326	-963099
Coptic	08 29, 284 AD	08 29, 284 AD	1825030	103605
Dies Torah	04 24, 3963 BC	03 23, 3963 BC	273686	-1447738
Diocletian	08 29, 283 AD	08 28, 283 AD	1824664	103638
Egyptian	02 26, 747 BC	02 18, 746 BC	1448638	-272787
Ethiopian	08 29, 8 AD	08 27, 8 AD	1724221	2796
Fasli	05 24, 600 AD	05 26, 600 AD	1940350	219325
French Rev	09 11, 1792 AD	09 22, 1792 AD	2375840	654415
Greek	06 21, 776 BC	06 10, 776 BC	1437793	-283232
Gregor. RD	01 03, 1 AD	01 01, 1 AD	1721425	1
Gregorian	10 05, 1582 AD	10 15, 1582 AD	2299161	577736
Hebrew	10 07, 3760 BC	09 07, 3760 BC	347998	-1373427
Hezekiah 14	03 13, 715 BC	03 05, 715 BC	1459976	-261449

Calendar	Julian	Gregorian	J.D.	R.D.
Islamic	07 16, 622 AD	07 19, 622 AD	1948440	227015
ISO	01 03, 1 AD	01 01, 1 AD	1721424	1
Julian Actual	01 01, 1 AD	12 30, 0 AD	1712927	-1
Julian Prolep	01 01, 4713 BC	11 24, 4713 BC	1	-1721424
Julian Sothic	07 19, 2782 BC	06 24, 2782 BC	705131	-1015895
Kali-Yuga	02 18, 3102 BC	01 23, 3101 BC	588466	-1132959
Khwarizmian	06 21, 632 AD	06 24, 632 AD	1952060	230635
Lillian Day	10 05, 1582 AD	10 15, 1582 AD	2299161	577737
Macedonian	09 01, 312 BC	08 27, 312 BC	1607709	-113716
Mayan	09 06, 3114 BC	08 11, 3113 BC	584283	-1137142
Nabonassar	02 25, 747 BC	02 14, 747 BC	1448269	-272756
Persian Orig	03 03, 389 BC	02 26, 388 BC	1579402	-141623
Persian	03 19, 622 AD	03 22, 622 AD	1948321	226896
Rata Die	01 03, 1 AD	01 01, 1 AD	1721426	1
Roman Orig	04 21, 753 BC	04 12, 753 BC	1446500	-274925
Saka	03 04, 79 AD	03 02, 79 AD	1749975	28570
Seleucid	10 07, 312 BC	10 02, 312 BC	1607745	-113680
Syrian	10 01, 312 BC	09 26, 312 BC	1607349	-113686
Teutonic				
Tibetan	12 10, 127 BC	12 07, 127 BC	1675015	-46410
Zoroastrian	06 16, 632 AD	06 19, 632 AD	1952063	230638

The basic algorithm is as follows:

> Calendar 1 (date) is converted to a Julian Day Count or Rata Die count

This day is then used to convert to the date in Calendar 2.

This algorithm works great between modern calendars, but when converting ancient calendars which had differing day counts for the year (i.e. 360 day versus 365 day), it could be seen that the calendars would *float* through one calendar or the other.

Less accurate in one sense, but more accurate when considering the astronomy of the seasons between two calendars is to use a day of the year count in both calendars, starting with a given point that both calendars can be matched to, such as the Spring Equinox or the Autumnal Equinox. The days are counted for the dates of both calendars from these starting points and them matched. This algorithm prevents floating so that a summer date in one calendar will still be a summer date in the other calendar.

> Day of the Year of Calendar 1 for the date in question is counted from the agreed starting point.

> The same starting point of Calendar 2 is found and the number of days added to this starting point that were

found in Calendar 1. This gives a close proximity date in Calendar 2, but isn't always an accurate date.

Ultimately, the truth lies in the fact that any historian that is matching dates between calendars from the ancient worlds has NO right to claim absolute accuracy. It isn't possible. Those prophetic interpreters who use extreme equations to show how a prophetic event fell at the appropriate time are no better than the soothsayers.

4. Recorded Time versus Pre-History: Historians do recognize the concept of recorded time and pre-recorded time, that time which is usually taking place in the Epochs of the earth before 4000 B.C. It is not within the scope of this work to discuss the Evolution Theory as that has been done in a previous work, "*Revised History of the Ancient World*" by Anthony Lyle. This work is limited to verifiable history through the Bible, recorded archaeological and ancient artifacts, and documents of manmade origin.

5. Determining the correct calendar to use with the Bible of this time: It isn't enough that we choose the right calendar from the perspective of getting the right number of days in a year. The start of the calendar has to align with certain events in the Bible where the day of the year and the day of the week are aligned as well.

Day counts for day of the week matches to day of the year: If the calendar in question doesn't match the 1st event of the Flood, then it becomes irrelevant if it matches the 2nd event and falls out (ignored). Iyyar 10, 1656 A.T. is the day that Noah was told to enter the ark. That day was a Shabbat. Iyyar 16, 2513 A.T. was the first day of manna after the Egyptian exodus, and fell on Sunday.

Calendar	Day count to Iyyar 10 1656	Day of Week	Day count to Iyyar 16 2513	Day of Week
360 / Nissan	595840	Shabbat	904366	Sunday
360 / Tishrei	596020	Thursday	Since none of these meet the first criteria of Shabbat for Iyyar 10, 1656 A.T., they cannot be qualified for the second criteria, leaving only one calendar system that works for the day counts.	
364 / Nissan	602460	Thursday		
364 / Tishrei	602640	Tuesday		
Hebrew / Nissan	604493	Sunday		
Hebrew / Tishrei	604685	Tuesday		
365.24 / Nissan	604516	Wednes.		
365.24 / Tishrei	604698	Wednes.		

There are two days given to us in the Bible that give both a day of year and a day of the week combination: The day that Noah entered the ark at the start of the deluge, (10th of Iyyar of 1656 A.M. which had to be a Shabbat or Sabbath or Saturday), and the day that manna started to fall after the Egyptian exodus (Iyyar 16, 2513 A.M.) which was a Sunday. The calendar needs to satisfy both of these conditions or it is not the right calendar. Below is a day count of many choices of calendars that could have existed at this ancient time. The Hebrew calendar is a modified version of the Metonic calendar created around 600 B.C. in Greece to account for both lunar and solar changes that had taken place around 700 B.C.

Following the Hebrew Calendar, the months are as follows for the Biblical Calendar Year until 715 B.C. when the earth changed its orbit:

Nissan 1 (Spring Equinox) – 30 days (month 1 according to this revised work). This is based on the Book of Esther which counted Nissan the first month and went to month 12, where the Jews were "supposed" to be killed in the month of Adar (12th month), and from Exodus where Nissan was specifically named as the first month.

Iyyar – 30 days
Tsivan – 30 days
Tammuz – 30 days
Av – 30 days
Elul – 30 days

Tishrei – 30days. This is the first month of the year according to Modern Hebrew Orthodox interpretation. They believe that the visitation of HaShem to Abraham took place in this month.

Marcheshvan – 30 days

Kislev – 30 days

Tevet – 30 days

Shevat – 30 days

Adar – 30 days (ends just before the Spring Equinox).

CHAPTER 2

AGE OF CREATION

6. Age of Creation: This work is based on the Masoretic Text of the Hebrew Bible. Many historians of Christian belief have tried to merge the history of the world with the Biblical events and most of them to complete failure. The problem was that they made the same mistake that this author made for the first 11 versions, and that is assuming that world history is correct and accurate. Throwing that premise away and starting with the Bible, it will be shown that the Bible and world history are perfectly aligned. This book will fit easily into the religious beliefs of the Jews, the Christians, and even the Muslims to a certain degree, as the ancient Muslims were Arabians, and closely associated with the Israelites, whether they wish to admit it or not. All three faiths have a belief in Abraham as the father of their beliefs.

This age starts with Day one of the Creation, which is relevant to all faiths. It is the age where HaShem creates the heavens and the earth. It is at this time that HaShem makes His first appearance on the surface of the earth: *The Spirit of HaShem hovered over the face of the deep (Gen/Bereshit 1:2).* According to Revelations, Yeshua ben Elohim was present at this time, but not as a human as we know Him. Anything that came before this age is considered to be the Alpha Period of HaShem. This age ends with the next visit of HaShem at the sin of Adam and Eve which resulted in the expulsion from the Garden of Eden.

6a. **First week of creation**: The seven days are considered by many liberal interpreters of the Bible as figurative and actually refer to the thousands of years before mankind appeared on the earth. Conservatives (orthodox) believe that they are literal days of night and day just as the Bible says, which does not allow any figurative language at all.

Alpha	Day 1	Day 2	Day 3	Day 4	Day 5	Day 6	Day 7	Omega	7 Days
	1000 Yrs	1000 Yrs	1000 Yrs	1000 Yrs	1000 Yrs	1000 Yrs	1000 Yrs		7000 Yrs
	20 Yovels	20 Yovels	20 Yovels	20 Yovels	20 Yovels	20 Yovels	20 Yovels		140 Yovels
	People before Abraham		Messianic Believers		Believers after Yeshua crucified				
	People who do not respond favorably to HaShem								

It is the interpretation of this work that the week of creation is both, figurative and literal. The literal days of 168 hours did take place as described, but they represent the next 7000 days of the work of HaShem throughout mankind. It is the belief here that HaShem has not hidden His plan or His works from us in mysteries, but rather right from the get-go told us what He planned on doing for the next 7000 years. This plan of HaShem is the guiding force behind this history work as it gives us a flow chart to follow to put history in proper place. Each day represents a thousand year period of our history. Right now, we are sitting about 20 years before the end of the 6th day or year 6000 A.T. (A.M. in the Hebrew chronology).

7. Genesis 1:1-5 (Bereshit 1:1-5): Day 1 of Creation: The first two verses give us the condition of the earth as HaShem created it in the first fraction of a second. The earth was without form, void, and darkness was upon the face of the deep. The first 2 verses indicates that the heavens and the earth were created at the same time, which directly contradicts Evolutionary Theories. This defines chaos, where everything was confusion and darkness. There were no Laws of Thermodynamics in existence because atomic or other forms of magnetism did not exist. The atomic particles floated around in a primordial soup not knowing how to interact to form atoms, and higher forms of physical structures. If we were to have been able to look down upon the universe at this instant, it would have been like trying to find a particular drop of water in a swimming pool of water, such was the earth in the universe at this moment. There was *no* light at all, which means that there was no photon activity, which means there was no atomic reactions taking place. What they lacked was the *knowledge of HaShem* which modern day scientists in their inability to understand has named magnetism.

Berossus: As quoted by Eusebius **gives a non**-Biblical description of the same point in time from the perspective of the Greeks: "*There was once a time, in which everything was darkness and water. In those times, monstrous beasts were born, with strange appearances. There were men with two wings, and some with four wings and two faces. They had one body, but two heads, of a man and a woman, and two sets of genitals, male and female. Other men had the legs and horns of a goat, or the hooves of a horse, or the rear end of a horse and the front of a man, like centaurs. Other beasts were born, such as bulls with human heads; dogs with four bodies and fish tails protruding from their rear end; horses with dogs' heads; humans and other animals with the head and body of a horse, but the tail of a fish; and other beasts with the form of all kinds of wild animals. As well as these [beasts], there were fish and reptiles and snakes and many other strange creatures, each of which had a different appearance. Representations of them were set up in the temple of Belus. A woman called Omorca ruled over all these [creatures]; she is called Thalatth in the Chaldean language, which is translated into Greek as thalassa ("the sea").*

Belus, which is translated as Zeus in Greek, cut the darkness in half. He separated the earth and the heavens from each other, and he arranged the universe. But because the creatures could not bear the power of the light, they were destroyed. When Belus saw that the land was empty and fertile, he ordered one of the gods to cut off his own head, and by mixing the blood which flowed from him with earth, to create men and wild beasts who could endure the air. Belus created the stars, the sun, the moon and the five planets."

7a. Date of Day 1: 0001.01.01 A.T. which translates to Nissan 1, 0001 Anno Torah or Year of Torah (A.T.) and 1 Dies Torah or Day Count of Torah (D.T.). This was Sunday, the first day of the week. The assigned / calculated day in the Gregorian calendar is March 22, 3963 B.C. (Sunday closest to Spring Equinox), Julian Day (J.D.) 273685. The equivalent date in the Hebrew or Jewish calendar is Elul 25, Year 0 Anno Mundi or Year of the World (A.M.). The Jews do not start their year 1 until the creation of Adam on the 6th day of the week. This results in a 5 day existence before time or when time didn't matter to them.

The calculation used in this work for finding Day 1 is based on counting backwards from the Crucifixion of Yeshua Messiah on Nissan

15, 4000 A.T. (a date that we can know for a certain). James Ussher (the first translator of the Bible into the King James English in the 1600's) used a similar method to calculate Day 1 of creation but he used the Birth of Christ instead of the Crucifixion. This results in a 37 year difference between his calculation and the concluded date in this work.

The day of His Crucifixion is based on Daniel who gave us when He was cut off after 483 years from the decree of Artaxerxes. 483 + 446 B.C. results in the year 37 A.D. for the crucifixion, which is exactly 4000 years after the creation. 4000 A.T. = 37 A.D. according to this work. 4000 – 37 = 3963 and then remembering that we chose the Sunday closest to the Spring Equinox brings us to Mar 22, 3963 B.C. as the first day of creation.

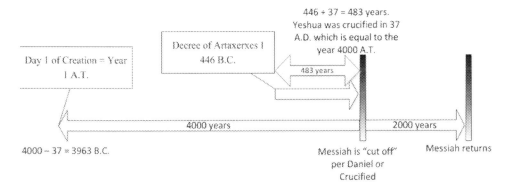

Besides, James Ussher, there have been many historians who have attempted the same feat of determining the first day of creation. Following is a chart of those calculations.

All dates before 4713 B.C. are based on the Septuagint version of the Bible which offers more years than the Masoretic Text (the orthodox version of Hebrew scholars and the chosen orthodox version used in this work). The Julian Day or Dies Torah day cannot be determined from the historians offering only a year of creation. The Seder Olam is the orthodox Hebrew history written in the early years after the crucifixion by Hebrew sages. The Sedar Olam is still used today as their basic history, even though they now recognize it is 202 years in error.

Historian	Gregorian B.C.	Julian Day	Rata Die	Dies Torah
Seder Olam	Feb 29, 3759	348173	-1372852	6
Hebrew Chronol.	Oct 2, 3761	347657	-1373368	6
Demetrius	5307			
Eupolemus	5307			
Hippolytus	5502			
Julius Africanus	5495			
James Ussher	Sep 21, 4004	259258	-1461767	-31821
Joseph Scaliger	3949			
Frank Klassen	Mar 1, 3975	269614	-1451411	-21465
Down / Ashton	3958			
David Rohl	5375			
Revised	Mar 22, 3963	273685	-1447340	1

The revised Gregorian is a "best guess" date against the Julian / Gregorian calendar. BeHaRD falls on the first lunation on Tishrei 2nd 1 A.M. in the Hebrew A.M. calendar.

Creation Week	1st Day	2nd Day	3rd Day	4th Day	5th Day	6th Day	Shabbat
Hebrew A.M.	Elul 25, 0 A.M.	Elul 26, 0	Elul 27, 0	Elul 28, 0	Elul 29, 0	Tishrei 1, 1 A.M.	Tishrei 2, 1
Hebrew Greg.	Oct 3	Oct 4	Oct 5	Oct 6	Oct 7	Oct 8	Oct 9
Revised A.T.	Nissan 1, 1 A.T.	Nissan 2	Nissan 3	Nissan 4	Nissan 5	Nissan 6	Nissan 7
Revised Greg.	Mar 22, 3963 BC	Mar 23	Mar 24	Mar 25	Mar 26	Mar 27	Mar 28

Creation Week	Winter	Spring	Summer	Fall	Winter	Spring	Summer	Fall
Hebrew A.M.	0 A.M.			1 A.M.				2 A.M.
James Ussher	4005 B.C.			4004 B.C.				4003 B.C.
Frank Klassen	3976 B.C.				3975 B.C.			
Revised		0 A.T.				1 A.T.		
Hebrew B.C.	3761 B.C.			3760 B.C.				3759
Revised Greg.	3964 B.C.			3963 B.C.				

Epochs of different calendars (first day of each calendar)

Calendar	Julian	Gregorian	J.D.	R.D.
Alexandrian	09 20, 23 BC	09 26, 23 BC	1712927	-8098
Anc. Babylon	03 23, 2241 BC	03 04, 2241 BC	902614	-818811
Anc. Egypt	03 14, 2148 BC	02 25, 2148 BC	936574	-784851
Armenian	07 11, 552 AD	07 13, 552 AD	1922868	201443
Armenian, Lit	08 11, 1084 AD			
Astronomical	12 19, 1999 AD	01 01 2000 AD	2451545	730121
Aztec	08 13, 1521 AD	08 22, 1521 AD	2276827	555403
Baha'i	03 11, 1844 AD	03 21, 1844 AD	2394710	673222
Celtic				
Chinese	03 08, 2637 BC	02 15, 2636 BC	758326	-963099
Coptic	08 29, 284 AD	08 29, 284 AD	1825030	103605
Dies Torah	04 24, 3963 BC	03 23, 3963 BC	273686	-1447738
Diocletian	08 29, 283 AD	08 28, 283 AD	1824664	103638
Egyptian	02 26, 747 BC	02 18, 746 BC	1448638	-272787
Ethiopian	08 29, 8 AD	08 27, 8 AD	1724221	2796
Fasli	05 24, 600 AD	05 26, 600 AD	1940350	219325
French Rev	09 11, 1792 AD	09 22, 1792 AD	2375840	654415
Greek	06 21, 776 BC	06 10, 776 BC	1437793	-283232
Gregor. RD	01 03, 1 AD	01 01, 1 AD	1721425	1
Gregorian	10 05, 1582 AD	10 15, 1582 AD	2299161	577736
Hebrew	10 07, 3760 BC	09 07, 3760 BC	347998	-1373427
Hezekiah 14	03 13, 715 BC	03 05, 715 BC	1459976	-261449

Calendar	Julian	Gregorian	J.D.	R.D.
Islamic	07 16, 622 AD	07 19, 622 AD	1948440	227015
ISO	01 03, 1 AD	01 01, 1 AD	1721424	1
Julian Actual	01 01, 1 AD	12 30, 0 AD	1712927	-1
Julian Prolep	01 01, 4713 BC	11 24, 4713 BC	1	-1721424
Julian Sothic	07 19, 2782 BC	06 24, 2782 BC	705131	-1015895
Kali-Yuga	02 18, 3102 BC	01 23, 3101 BC	588466	-1132959
Khwarizmian	06 21, 632 AD	06 24, 632 AD	1952060	230635
Lillian Day	10 05, 1582 AD	10 15, 1582 AD	2299161	577737
Macedonian	09 01, 312 BC	08 27, 312 BC	1607709	-113716
Mayan	09 06, 3114 BC	08 11, 3113 BC	584283	-1137142
Nabonassar	02 25, 747 BC	02 14, 747 BC	1448269	-272756
Persian Orig	03 03, 389 BC	02 26, 388 BC	1579402	-141623
Persian	03 19, 622 AD	03 22, 622 AD	1948321	226896
Rata Die	01 03, 1 AD	01 01, 1 AD	1721426	1
Roman Orig	04 21, 753 BC	04 12, 753 BC	1446500	-274925
Saka	03 04, 79 AD	03 02, 79 AD	1749975	28570
Seleucid	10 07, 312 BC	10 02, 312 BC	1607745	-113680
Syrian	10 01, 312 BC	09 26, 312 BC	1607349	-113686
Teutonic				
Tibetan	12 10, 127 BC	12 07, 127 BC	1675015	-46410
Zoroastrian	06 16, 632 AD	06 19, 632 AD	1952063	230638

7b. ***"In the beginning, God…"*** The Christian concept of HaShem (i.e. the Trinity) was based on the conclusions of the Council of Nicaea in 325 B.C. A particular sect was trying to argue that Yeshua was not God but a normal human. The Trinity definition that resulted from the council determined to become the orthodox view of God in the Christian world is God, the Father, God, the Son, and God, the Holy Spirit. This is not the orthodox view of the Hebrews. Deuteronomy 6:4 contradicts the trinity perception: *"YHWH elohanu, YHWH echad"* (Jehovah is our God, Jehovah is ONE). The orthodox view of the Hebrews is the view taken in this work, but not the Arian view that Yeshua was *just* a man. He was God in Man, the Son of the Living God, above other humans in that He did not sin and thus died on the cross an innocent man.

7c. **Condition of the universe in Verse 2**: As mentioned, the universe in verse 2 indicates that the universe that existed was just a primordial soup or watery form. Clarence Larkin believes that verse 2 was the result of things that went bad after verse 1. Then in verse 3, God *recreated the heavens and the earth*. This conclusion is rejected here. Verse 1 is a summary and verse 2 is the condition of the heavens and the earth in the first *moment of time*.

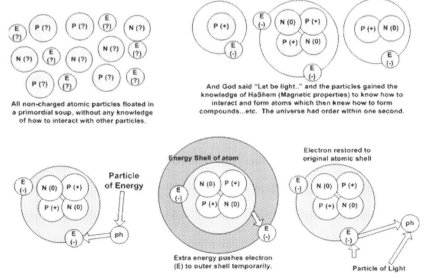

All non-charged atomic particles floated in a primordial soup, without any knowledge of how to interact with other particles.

And God said "Let be light.." and the particles gained the knowledge of HaShem (Magnetic properties) to know how to interact and form atoms which then knew how to form compounds…etc. The universe had order within one second.

Energy Shell of atom

Particle of Energy

Extra energy pushes electron (E) to outer shell temporarily.

Electron restored to original atomic shell

Particle of Light

And God said "Let be light..". This set of 3 pictures shows that light was defined on day 1, not by the sun but by the atomic reactions of energy to matter, i.e. photons (ph) and electron (E) energy shells (shown as different shades of gray).

7d. **Verse 3: *"Light be."*** This is a more direct translation of the Hebrew words in the Masoretic text. It was a command from HaShem. The word used for light has multiple meanings, but the one important to us is the knowledge of God. Light is just one translation, but this translation has led to the confusion that the light that was created was of a planetary level. The light that was truly created was more at an atomic level, giving particles in the primordial soup the *knowledge* of how to interact with other particles, I.e. magnetism! Magnetism is a scientific word assigned to the knowledge of HaShem by men who do not understand or do not believe in a supreme being. This light/knowledge was given to the particles and an explosion took place across the universe as particles exhibited the feature of Quantum Physics called Collective Knowledge of a species. The species in this case is atomic and compound particles. The explosion expanded the universe in seconds by using electrical and chemical processes (De Grazia and Milton). It is proposed here that the universe reached 75% of its current size in the first second of creation (a counter theory to the theory of evolution). This explosion does support the *Big Bang* theory of many scientists as it was a huge explosion of proportions beyond our comprehension.

8e. **The day is defined**: It is here in verses 4 and 5 that this work defines the day as a period of darkness followed by a period of light (dusk to dusk day).

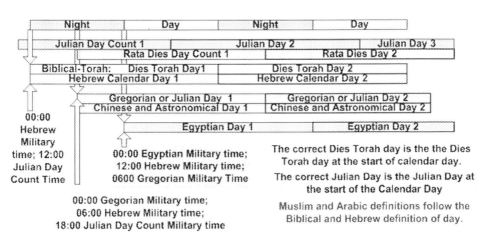

8. Bereshit / Genesis 1:6-8: Day 2: The date is given as Nissan 2, 0001 A.T. Monday or March 23, 3963 B.C. (J.D. 273686). At this point, there are no stars or planets except earth. This is a particular point of conflict for evolution believers who believe that planets came about through slow processes of gravity collecting particles from space until their relative size was that of a planet or star. There is also no mention of heaven and hell, although some extra-biblical Hebrew sources (*Haggadah)* indicate that they were created *before* the physical entities of earth and space. The Big Bang of day 1 has created a vast space between the *waters above and the waters below.* The waters below are the waters on the face of the earth. The waters above is a definition of the area *beyond the universe.* The space between will be the universal ether that will hold billions of stars and planets.

9. Bereshit/Genesis 1:9-13: The date is given as Nissan 3, 0001 A.T. or 3 D.T. The equivalent Gregorian date is March 24, 3963 B.C. Tuesday. The land exploded out of the waters. This would make one of our top earthquakes look like a mere rumble in the earth. Velikovsky and John C. Whitcomb, and Henry M. Morris (*"The Genesis Flood")* indicate that the water tables were about 2 miles lower at this time than they are in our current world. The sandbars located 2 miles below the surface of the water is evidence of this lower water table as sand only accumulates at the edges of larger areas of water. This would lead us to believe that the lands that existed at this time were not divided by waters but interconnected so that when the animals were created, they would be able to go anywhere in the world without restriction. Apparently plants were created but from verses later on it is believed that they were created as seeds and did not appear immediately.

The Jewish thought is that the Garden of Eden was created this day, but the orthodox Bible indicates that it might not have been created until after Adam was created. David Rohl believes he found the Garden of Eden located just west of the Caspian Sea on the east side of Mesopotamia. He believes that Ezekiel provided the clue (Ezekiel 28: 11-19) when he says it is inside the *mountain of God.* Lucifer was found there among the rocks of fire (lava).

10. Bereshit / Genesis 1: 14-19: The date is given as Nissan 4, 0001 A.T. or D.T. 4, also as March 25, 3963 B.C. (J.D. 273688) or Wednesday. The Hebrew language has words that differentiate planets from stars, and earth from moon. None of these words were used. It is the opinion here, that HaShem used *exact language to indicate what He meant* in the verses. All we know is that 2 great lights were placed in the sky. They were not planets. It is the conclusion here that on this day, the universe consisted of 2 stars and earth. Nothing more.

Alfred De Grazia and Milton believes that our solar system bears a strong resemblance to a Two Star system. Having reviewed the ancient mythologies, not as religious documents but as eyewitness accounts of the past, they believe that the mythologies are exactly that, eyewitness accounts of what happened in the heavens above. It is a mystery as to why in the ancient mythologies almost all cultures chose Uranus to be the main god, when it is obvious to our modern world that the sun is much larger. It is De Grazia's conclusion that the second star of this day was Uranus, not as a planet but as a star that was much closer to earth than the sun and therefore *appeared* to be larger. This smaller size would explain why the heat from this star did not burn the earth up, aside from protection from supernatural forces (i.e. HaShem). The earth was held between the two stars, both earth and Uranus still circling the much larger light of the sun. The earth was not in constant light as attested by the previous verses of a rotation of the earth leading to darkness and light upon the surface of the earth.

The two star solar system as pictured by De Grazia and Milton

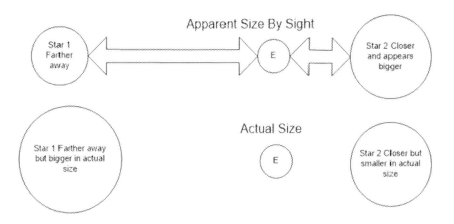

10a. **Ancient mythology as evidence**: Helios, the sun god of the ancient Greeks (and other cultures by a different name) did not become

one of the main gods until well late in human written history. Practically every culture of a multi-god system had Uranus as the first god, Saturn as the second, and followed by Jupiter as the main gods. Even more surprising is that the other gods (Neptune, Pluto, and Mercury) were known by the ancients, even though visibly they are beyond our normal vision in space. The ancients did not have telescopes (invented in the 1400's A.D.). It is apparent from the ancient mythologies that the people on earth were able to see these planets at some point. They were able to see the rings of Saturn, and the two steeds of Mars, and the sons and daughters (moons) of Jupiter. Ancient mythologies indicate that Uranus *ate* his children until Saturn / Kronos over threw him. This is evidence that the solar system has not been stable for millions of years as indicated by scientists, historians, and devout evolution believers. These solar changes took place within the lives of ancient people, ancient *written history.*

11. Bereshit / Genesis 1:20-21: The date is Nissan 5, 0001 A.T. or Thursday. This is calculated as March 26, 3963 B.C. 273689 J.D. This is the day before the Hebrew calendar officially begins. Sea Creatures and flying creatures are created. This defies evolution concepts that the sea creatures took millions of years to evolve into flying creatures, amphibians, and eventually land crawlers. The theories developed by Darwin (who did not believe in Evolution) suggest that natural selection takes a large number of years for a species to change, but laws of genetics are seldom violated in this process. This means that DNA of a species limits procreation between different species. Humans have never been able to have Chimpanzee children.

11a. DNA: There are 4 types of DNA *particles* as it were. These DNA particles form strands that control the outcome of species development from conception (be it plant or animal) to maturity. The particles are paired but genetic scientists have deduced that the DNA strands are a form of computer code only not in binary. Rather they are quaternary code sequences that will allow some cross procreating but not between different species. It forms a complex double binary code.

11b. Sea Monsters: Ancients give evidence of huge sea monsters having existed in the beginning before men were created. Alexander Apollodorus describes huge creatures in the very beginning of existence. His original descriptions have been lost in translation, being 3rd generation translations from Berossus.

12. Bereshit / Genesis 1:24-27 (2:5-9): The date is Nissan 6, 0001 A.T. Dies Torah 6 on Friday. The Gregorian Date is March 27, 3963 B.C. J.D. 273690 (Friday). This is the first day of the Hebrew Calendar, Tishrei 1, 0001 A.M. 348171 J.D. The Julian day does not match the A.T. date here due to the difference in the year of the Gregorian Epoch. While this is considered their first day, this day is proleptic in that their current calendar wasn't created until after 600 B.C. The Hebrew calendar is a Metonic based calendar with some modifications (extra rules to prevent holidays from being next to a Shabbat). There is not one document in the Hebrew catalogue that supports a Hebrew calendar in existence before 700 B.C.

12a. Animals are categorized into 3 divisions: cattle, creeping things, and beasts. Not all the species alive today was necessary in the beginning. While DNA prevents cross breeding of a species, it doesn't prevent within a species. This is where Darwin's Theory of Natural Selection comes in. The species will adapt to the changes in the environment and subtle differences within a species will be created: Doberman instead of a German Shepard, Gray Fox instead of a Red Fox, different versions of chickens, etc.

12b. Adam: The word even means man in Hebrew, and in particular, it means red man. This would indicate that the first man was not really white, but rather of an Indian or Middle East race. Later, the word Cush is used to mean black man, and one of Ham's sons was named Cush. In China, the first ruler was a black man (according to the Bamboo Archives). In the Western part of China, white men were found to be mummified under natural circumstances in the very early history of China. Oriental appearances did appear early in the China's history and the third ruler of China was oriental in appearance.

12c. First woman: The Masoretic text and the King James Bible tell us that Eve was taken from Adam, but there is absolutely no verbiage to indicate that she was the first woman. Both merely say that she was taken from Adam to be his helpmate.

There are extra-Biblical books that tell us that the first woman was Lilith. She is mentioned in Isaiah, the *Song of the Sages (one of the Dead Sea scrolls), Book of Gigas, Zohar, Haggadah,* and finally in the *Epic of*

Gilgamesh. In all references she is not depicted in a good light. Rabbi Isaac Ben Jacob says that Lilith was the wife of Samael, (Satan or Lucifer). In Sumerian, Lilith's name uses the root Lil, which is a core part of Enlil, the false Sumerian god (probably another name for Samael in Sumerian). In Babylonian mythology, she is Lilu, or Lilit and is the first vampire feeding mainly on sleeping children. She is mentioned in the Talmud (Shabbat 151b), which indicates that Adam procreated through her and had male and female demons born to her. The Muslim view of Lilith is that she was of Jewish origin and there is some doubt in the Islamic Faith as to her reality, but she is mentioned in extra-Islamic texts. However, those that do believe in Lilith believe that she and Satan spawned Djinn or demons. In Muslim myth, she is named Hawwa, which is the name given to Eve as well. Hawwa is also the name of the god that was being hunted by Gilgamesh. Unlike the demons of Jewish / Christian origin, these demons have the ability to be either good or evil. In this mythology, Adam returned to Eve before the birth of Seth. Neither Lilith nor Eve was made in the first week. Adam was alone when he named the animals. Islamic tradition indicates that Eve died around 3070 B.C., 1 year after Adam. They believe that she gave birth 20 times, each time with twins (1 boy and 1 girl).

If Lilith exists (and this work only recognizes the many ancient records of her existence, but does not purport that she did actually exist), she turned from Adam after Satan's rebellion from HaShem. She married Samael and is later reported to have mated with Cain ben Adam (son of Adam) as well.

Creation of Adam, Lilith, and Eve: Waddell believes this ancient seal dated around 2300 B.C. is about the trial of Adam. This revised interpretation believes that it shows the ancient belief that Adam was created as a twofold creature, male and female. Once Lilith was her own person, she rebelled. She is shown with the feet of birds, which is a very typical illustration of Lilith in archaeology. Following her rebellion Adam is shown to the right along with Eve. The figure to the far left is HaShem, or Ia (God of the Semites) and he made the stars in the sky. The circles are symbols of ancient Babylon to depict male, or female. The creature below Lilith represents her demon creatures.

13. First two rules or commandments: Adam was told to replenish the earth. The wording here is what gives Clarence Larkin ammunition to support a previous earth theory indicating that replenish means to restore human life on earth after it was somehow lost. The word can also mean just to procreate life on earth. The second rule was to avoid eating from the Tree of Knowledge of Good and Evil. The Tree of Life seems to have been fair game, but it is apparent that they did not eat of the Tree of Life during their stay in Eden. Some seminaries believe this is a covenant, but there is no sign given that usually accompanies a covenant with HaShem. This commandment was given to Adam *before Eve was created. It was given only to Adam.*

The Quran follows the creation of Adam and Eve very closely. To Muslims, Adam was the first true prophet of Islam. The garden was not named or described in the Quran. Eve is not named Eve in the Quran.

13a. Garden: It had not yet rained on the earth, and the plants were watered from the natural mists. The plants didn't grow until man was there to work the ground and take care of the garden. The two trees were figurative, but also literal as shown in Genesis 3. They represent the single most important choice in a person's life, to obey HaShem and get life, or to disobey and fall into sin.

14. Bereshit / Genesis 1:29-2:4: The date is Nissan 7, 0001 A.T. or 7 D.T. The Gregorian date is March 28, 3963 B.C. Saturday, J.D. 273691. The Hebrew date is Tishrei 2, 0002 A.M. and they also give this day as a

Saturday. HaShem blessed the 7th day and everything that he had made. This blessing included Adam.

This is the Shabbat and in figurative language this day represents the Kingdom Age where Yeshua rules at absolute King over the earth, the last 1000 years of history. We are fast approaching that period of time as we end 6000 years of history. HaShem rested mainly because His Son rules over the earth. Satan is bound in Perdition for 1000 years.

The verse reads that up to this point, 7 days, *everything* is good. This refers to the literal time period now, not the figurative. This includes Satan and Lilith. They had not yet rebelled against HaShem or Adam. The sin of Adam and Eve had not yet taken place. There were no poisonous plants or animals. Everything was peaceful. Creation of mankind is complete. The Tractate Shabbat of Babylonian Talmud defines Shabbat as the *cessation of wrath.* This fits well with our interpretation of the 6000 years of history, which ends with 50 years of the wrath of HaShem before the return of our Savior. The next 7000 years will be HaShem's cessation from His wrath.

14a. Blessing from HaShem is forever. Once blessed, one cannot be cursed. Anyone attempting to curse a blessed person ends up with the curse reverting back to them. Abraham was one such blessed that his blessing was eternal and anyone who curses Abraham is himself (herself) cursed.

15. **Bereshit / Genesis 2:18-25**: Eve is created as a helpmate to Adam. She was given to Adam right after he finished naming the creatures of the lands and air. He did not give names to the creatures of the sea. These verses give rise to the idea that the animals of the land were created after Adam, not before, on the 6th day. After the woman was made, Adam then named her as well as woman (Ishshah, which is derived from the Hebrew word for man, Ish.). The two of them were naked and didn't realize it. This is often referred to as the Dispensation of Innocence by dispensationalists.

15a. The date for this event is not given. It takes place shortly after the 7th day, or Shabbat Day. Since the garden was able to sprout forth plants, this time is very open to interpretation. The event of Eve's creation could have been a day after the 7th day, a week, or many weeks. If Lilith existed in reality, her fall and turning away from Adam took place before the creation of Eve. The next chapter starts with the Serpent being evil, so this is after the blessing of the 7th day and before the creation of Eve. Both Even and

Adam were created with age intact, meaning that they were at least adults. This means that both of them were over the age of 13 and that's as close as we can discern. They were both through puberty and able to have sex and bear children.

15b. **An example of marriage**, in HaShem's eyes, Adam and Eve were man and wife. They were joined by HaShem, meaning it was Holy Marriage. There was no exchange of vows, and in fact, the traditional Jewish or Christian marriage ceremony cannot be found in the Bible at all. In Christian circles, the marriage ceremony is the product of the Anglican Church and became adapted by puritan believers.

In this union, there was no house to keep, no dishes to do, or laundry. Eve's function was to help Adam achieve the keeping of the garden. Nothing more. They worked together and accomplished the same end. Nor did they always work side by side. In the next chapter, Eve is apparently alone when approached by the serpent. While the first child does not appear to be born until after they are exiled from the garden, it is unknown if they cohabitated during their time in Eden. It is likely that they might have since one of the commandments given to Adam was to replenish the earth and Adam would have wanted to please his Lord.

15c. ***The Book of Enoch*** (*Book of Idris* in Muslim) believes that both Eve and Adam were created on day 6, but the verses taken chronologically between the creations of Adam, the blessing of the 7th day, the naming of the animals, and then the creation of Eve suggest otherwise. Eve was not part of the blessing on the 7th day as when HaShem punishes her for her sin, she is not blessed and is cursed in childbirth. Adam however, is not cursed for the same sin. Rather, the *earth* is cursed in his stead. Enoch states that they were in Eden exactly 5 hours, and 540 chalakim. Again, this could not be true as this would mean that they sinned on the 6th day and then HaShem would not have found *everything good on the 7th day*. The Haggadah agrees with Enoch.

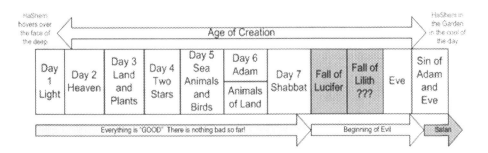

15d. *The Book of Jubilees* says that Adam wasn't allowed into Eden for 40 days, (the ritualistic requirement of cleansing of a new male according to the Law of Moses). Eve then had to wait for 80 days after her creation before being allowed to enter. Once again, this doesn't make sense. Adam was in the garden when she was created, so she would have been created in the garden already.

This lead to the following order of events: (1-9 are in the first *week*)

1-6, creation of the universe, earth, two lights, sea creatures, air creatures

7. Adam

8. Land Creatures

9. Shabbat is blessed by HaShem

10. Fall of Lucifer?

11. Fall of Lilith? (Myth or not, is unknown)

12. Creation of Eve

16. **Bereshit/Genesis 3:1-7: Temptation:** The time of the temptation by Satan is unknown, but is very likely soon after the creation of Eve. Adam had received the command to procreate and as of yet, they had not had time to do that, or Eve was just pregnant and we are not told that she was. The Quran does not indicate that Satan took the form of a Serpent. This is purely a Jewish/Christian part of the story, but it is the orthodox view of this work. The Serpent was in the Garden of Eden in the beginning (Ezekiel 28:11-19). Satan's beauty and power among the cherubs caused him to be haughty and full of pride. Lucifer was on the mountain of HaShem, just as David Rohl indicated when he found what he thinks is the Garden of Eden inside the crater of the mountain. Lucifer was forced from the mountain of HaShem and he was filled with violence. The use of fires

and rocks of fire are what we think of when we think of Lucifer and how he lives in a world (hell) of fire. He was made a terror to all that live upon the earth, including the beasts. If one has had demonic experience, they might have noticed the reactions of terror in the animals around them. *"The Book of Enoch"* says that Lucifer created Satan to fill the serpent. *"The Book of Jubilee"* called the spirit Gadrel. Lucifer committed the first sin (pride in his impossible thought of ruling over HaShem). This sin did not happen until after Adam and Eve were created as it specifically says that Lucifer was there in the Garden of Eden.

16a. Plan **of Satan:** Lucifer didn't just tempt Eve out of revengeful anger. He had a plan. He knew HaShem intimately before his fall. He knew that HaShem was a God of Justice and a God of Mercy. He played these two traits against one another. HaShem loved man, and if Lucifer could get man to sin, then HaShem's justice would either have to condemn man as Lucifer had been condemned or forgive man out of His merciful love. If he forgave man, the justice side of HaShem would prevail and He would be forced to forgive Lucifer as well. HaShem did both, He condemned man to death, but then paid the price of death through Yeshua.

The interesting thing is that Lucifer's words to Eve were true. They did not die on the day they ate of the fruit, (24 hour day). Lucifer has never been recorded telling a direct lie and yet he is considered the ultimate liar. His lies are not one of words, but one of motive. His motive was to separate Adam and Eve from HaShem. This is the worst lie and hard to detect. Someone can tell the truth, but if their *motive* is to deceive or degrade than their words are still false and they are a liar. The day that HaShem referred to in His warning was the 1000 year day. Adam and Eve both died around 930 A.T., during the *first millennial day*. Satan used the semantic difference to deceive Eve.

16b. **Loss of innocence:** Adam and Eve were not only able to directly communicate with HaShem but also with the animals before they lost their innocence. They lost that ability when they sinned, something that an animal cannot do. All animals have the same innocence from sin, and it is the premise here that they can communicate with HaShem on a basic level. Adam and Eve immediately saw that they were naked and *they were ashamed*. They knew they were naked before, but there was no shame in it.

17. **Bereshit 3:8-13: Results of their sin:** One of the unforeseen consequences was the loss of the deed to earth. Before they sinned, HaShem owned the deed to earth and they inherited it. When they sinned, they sold the earth to Satan. The significance of this is that only a kinsman can redeem the deed during the last year of yovel. In this case, Yeshua is our *Redeemer* and He has to redeem the deed on a Yovel. When Adam and Eve step out into the world and take possession of it, this starts the *first Yovel count*. This yovel ends in the year 6000 with the 120th Yovel. Yeshua will return in the year 6000 A.T. to redeem the deed to earth. This coincides with the binding of Satan for 1000 years.

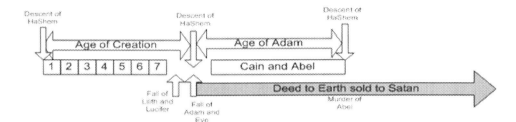

17a. **HaShem descends to earth for 2nd time**: This action of HaShem is the result of sin and He confronts Adam and Eve on their sin. He gave them every chance to defend themselves, but instead, they blame someone else. Adam blames Eve and Eve blames the Serpent. This does not do any good. If we are to define Ages by the actions of HaShem, then this one starts a new *Age.* It is a short age, ending with the murder of Abel by his brother Qayan (Cain).

One of the other consequences of their sin was *terror of Hashem.* Before this, they had no reason or ability to fear HaShem. Now, when HaShem is wandering in the garden in the cool of the day, they hide from him. HaShem calls out to them, knowing that they are afraid and He knows why.

18. **Bereshit 3:14-19: The Consequences of Sin:** The serpent was punished first, and was not given a chance to make excuses. The serpent, which was formerly a beautiful creature with limbs. He was cursed to crawl upon the ground in the dust. The Islam tradition does not put Satan in the

form of a serpent, but directly as himself. Some Jewish traditions indicate that Satan put *Lucifer* into the serpent.

The curse in the Jewish tradition is a prediction of the coming Savior, Yeshua Messiah. All three major faiths believe in the Messiah, but the Christian and Muslim religions believe that Yeshua the Crucified was the Messiah. The Jewish Faith is waiting for the Messiah to appear. This prediction goes along with the belief of this work that HaShem is not a God of mystery but is a God of *full disclosure* telling us what is going to take place.

18a. **Eve:** The punishment of Eve was twofold and the duality of it is a conflict for the woman. The first part is the extreme pain that comes with childbirth. The second part of the punishment is the desire or lust for her husband is increased. In other words, while childbirth is painful, the strongest desire a woman has is sex. Worse, this lust will rule over the woman (the verses have been interpreted to mean that the man will rule over the woman, but the verse is specific to the lust). There is no separation between the strong desire and the rule over the woman.

Lucifer was able to deceive her through her desire to be like HaShem. He deceived her into thinking that not only would she not die (today) but she would be like the Most High, something that Lucifer himself ascribed to be.

18b. **Adam:** Adam's sin was to listen to Eve tempt him to disobey HaShem. His sin was twofold; to listen to temptation against HaShem and to eat that which HaShem ordered him not to. Yet, Adam had been blessed on the 7th Day, the Shabbat. He could not be cursed. In his stead, the earth was cursed. Balaam is an excellent example of this rule of blessing and cursing. When the king hired him to curse Israel, he tried 3 times to curse Jacob but was not allowed by HaShem to do so, because Israel was blessed through Abraham. The ground was cursed so that when man tried to till it, it would bring forth weeds and thorns (another prediction about the crown of thorns place on the head of the Savior when He was crucified). This curse meant that the work that was formerly easy for Adam, would now be hard labor to get past the thorns and weeds. The final part of his punishment was that of a physical death, which applies to all men, born of dust and to dust they return. This is called the *first* death.

18c. Deed to Earth: Adam had formerly held the deed to the earth, the land of the earth bestowed upon him by HaShem. In Jewish Law, once the lands of Israel were allotted, they were to stay with a family generation after generation. A family could *temporarily* sell the deed to the land to another, even another in a different tribe and the new owner of the deed would reap the results of the land. The one condition to this was given in the Law of the Yovel. Each Yovel, all deeds would return to the original owner, *if there was someone in the original family to claim that deed back (kinsman).* Adam sold the earth deed to Satan and the result is as we have seen in history, Satan reaping the results of the earth and all men by their sin, their violence, their sexual depravity, and all sorts of evil in the world. The deed of the earth is due to be taken back but only after the *work of HaShem is complete.* It is the premise here that this work will be complete in the figurative translation of the creation week of 6 days or a literal *6000 years.* At that time, 120 Yovels will have passed and our *Kinsman,* Yeshua the Messiah, will return to reclaim the deed and take the earth back. The year of His return will fall on a Yovel year (based on the Yovel of Adam). Whether His return falls on a Yovel of Israel is hard to say as the Yovel has become convoluted from the Israel perspective. Following this action, Satan is to be bound for 1000 years in the Lake of Fire and Yeshua will take His final title, that of King of Kings. The rules of the Yovel can be found in Deuteronomy. It is the premise here that the year of the world since creation is around 5980 A.T. (at the time of this writing), meaning we have about 20 years to go before this return. It is incidental that the Islam Faith, which also believes in Yeshua, also believes that the time of His return is very near. Due to a miscalculation of the Jewish history, their own calculations differ by 202 years, so they are not expecting the Messiah back anytime soon.

19. Bereshit 3:20-24: Banishment: Eve is named at this time. Before now she was simply Ishshah the woman mate of Adam. If anything, they were made more equal now than before. They were forced to work together, but not for HaShem. They would be forced to work together for survival. HaShem made their first garments out of skins, which means that a sacrifice of animal life had to take place (i.e., the spilling of blood). Their sin is covered by the loss of blood which is in itself a huge prediction of the coming Messiah, whose blood will cover the sins of all mankind. The garments could have been made from plants, but HaShem chose to make them out of animal skins to indicate the loss of life caused by their sin.

19a. **Eden**: In Eden, they still had the ability to take of the Tree of Life and attain immortality thus defeating the purpose of the consequences. HaShem says "...*man has become like one of us...*" The "*us*" refers to the heavenly beings, Himself and the angels, but does not imply that they had become like gods. Rather they had become like the heavenly beings knowing good and evil. Some Christian theologians indicate that this us refers to the Trinity of HaShem; Father, Son, and Holy Spirit. That is not the interpretation of this work.

They were put out of the garden, which tells us that the garden did not cover the face of the earth, but was a specific place on the earth. A cherubim (special type of angel) was place in the single entrance to the garden with the *fiery ever turning sword*. It does not say that the cherubim ever turned the sword, but that the sword itself was ever turning and fiery.

19b. **Cherubim**: This specific word for angels appears 3 times in the Pentateuch and 4 times in Isaiah. Only in Isaiah 6:2-6 does the context of this word mean angel. The other 3 times in Isaiah, it refers in context to serpents. Some scholars believe that the cherubim do not have the same status as all angels. Conservative and Reformed Jews do not take angels as literal, but believe they are figurative or symbolic. In Christian practice, they are the caretakers of HaShem's throne. Thomas Aquinas indicates that they are creatures of heat. Islam angels have no free will and must serve HaShem's demands. A true Islam believer must believe in angels as part of their articles of faith.

CHAPTER 3

AGE OF ADAM (BEGINNING OF WRITTEN HISTORY)

20. **Descendents of Adam and Eve: Bereshit / Genesis 4:1-15:** Qayan and Hebel (Cain and Abel) are born to Adam and Eve in this order. The exact date is unknown, but presumed to be the first 3 years after their exile; 1 – 3 A.T. or 3963-3961 B.C. The premise is based on the command of HaShem to procreate the earth (a command that is still in force even though they were exiled from Eden) and Eve's new sexual desire for her husband.

    20a. Cain: Louis Ginzberg believes that Satan deceived Eve yet again and it was he who conceived Cain through Eve. There is also an unnamed son conceived by Adam and Lilith in the Ginzberg's records. *The Book of Jubilees* has Cain being born around 64 A.T. *The Apocalypse of Moses* has him being born around 18 A.T. A noted Jewish Rabbi, Rashi, has Cain being born before the exile from Eden. The Baha'i view is the same that Cain was born in Eden, 3950 B.C. Cain was a farmer of the earth like his father.

    20b. **Abel**: *The Book of Adam and Eve* has Abel being born 3 years after Cain. This is the only reference to Abel in all of the Hebrew texts. Islam views Abel as a prophet, like his father. Abel was a sheepherder.

    20c. **Offering to HaShem:** Jumping forward some 16 to 20 years, (exact time is not given), the two are required to offer sacrifices. The Islam tradition indicates that this was to determine which of the two women would be their wives (based on the fact that the prettiest one would go to the winner), (the women being twin sisters of each of the brothers). When Abel's sacrifice was taken (burned by fire of HaShem) he got the choice wife of the two available women. This is the Islam reason for Cain's anger.

The Torah/Bible does not really say why Cain's sacrifice was not acceptable, but this work believes it was because Cain's sacrifice was not of blood, which is the only acceptable sacrifice for sins, (looking forward again to the sacrifice of Yeshua for the sins of all mankind through His blood). Grain sacrifices are found in the Law of Moses, so it could not be that grain sacrifices were always rejected by HaShem. Grain sacrifices do have a particular time of year in the Law for their acceptance, so it might be that the time of the year was not acceptable for Cain's grain sacrifice. There is the possibility that Cain's sacrifice was an offering *to the earth* which is witchcraft and therefore unacceptable by HaShem, but there is no indication that Cain was a worshipper of the earth since his sacrifice was to appease HaShem. It is clear in verses 6-7, that the sacrifice was not rejected by HaShem due to some anger toward Cain by HaShem. HaShem even warns Cain not to be angry or the anger would lead to sin.

The offering of Cain was mentioned by Menes, son of Sargon I, also called Manas-tishu and the first Pharaoh of Egypt's Dynasty 1. His inscriptions can be found on the walls of Sippar. They were found by H. Rassam in 1881-82 AD. This is a credible archaeological record that supports the Biblical narrative.

20d. **First recorded murder**: It is not clear that the murder of Abel took place immediately after the sacrifice. Given the Islam view of the sacrifices being used to dictate which wife Abel would get, it would be logical to assume that the murder did take place soon after the sacrifice as Abel had no children, meaning he didn't live long enough to conceive through his wife. It is known for certain that Abel was killed with a rock (Jeremiah 17:9). Cain was married by the time of the murder. The murder took place before the birth of Seth as Eve referred to Seth as a *replacement* for her lost son, Abel.

It is important to note that between verse 7 and verse 8, some time passed, although how much is unknown. This is prevalent through the Bible as many times it would *appear* that time is immediate between verses, when in reality, time often passes between one verse and the one following. There is no indication of the amount of time between Bereshit 4:7 and Bereshit 4:8 (Genesis 4:7, 8). Then again more time between verse 8 and 9.

Islam suggests that Cain didn't know what to do with the body, but a crow came (was sent by HaShem) carrying another dead crow and the live crow began to bury the dead crow, thus educating Cain (or Adam) on what to do with the body. The Orthodox Jewish tradition indicates that Cain immediately buried the body to hide it from HaShem.

20e. **Curse of Cain:** The body of Abel had already been buried when HaShem descends for the 3rd time to deal with sin again, the sin of Cain. HaShem questions Cain about Abel who denies everything. HaShem then confronts Cain with the blood of the earth calling out the crime. This causes Cain to be *more cursed than the ground*. Cain lost his livelihood in farming and was not able to farm again. He became a wanderer. Cain was also banished from the presence of HaShem, losing all contact or communication with the Supreme Creator.

The mark placed on Cain has been conjectured throughout time but no one has real knowledge about that mark. A horn on his head has been suggested, but the most prevalent belief is the change of his skin to black. This would explain why Cush, son of Ham, was a black man and how black men lived when Adam and Eve were of Middle Eastern color.

The *mark of Cain* is not the same thing as the *curse of Cain*. Thus attributing a black skin color to being cursed of Hashem is a false racial projection. The *mark of Cain* was a *protective* symbol to warn others against harming Cain. Another conjecture is that Cain became a leper or an albino which would also stand out among a people of tanned skin. Miriam, the sister of Moses, was marked with leprosy (white skin) after she spoke against Moses for having married a Cushite (black woman). The *Way of Cain* is said to be a mark of Cain, Jude 10, 11, which is a way of *anger*.

CHAPTER 4

AGE OF CAIN

21. **Bereshit / Genesis 4:16-18: Nod:** The fear of Cain was that people around the world would hunt him now as being an outcast of HaShem. This fear leads to a logical conclusion that the world was already populated with a number of people, obvious brothers and sisters of Cain and Abel. It is stated later that Adam had other sons and daughters. In Hebrew, the word *Nod* means "wanderer, exile, and fugitive". *The Second Book of Adam and Eve* tells us that the name of Cain's wife was Luluwa (Lilith, which could be where the idea of Lilith originated). This book tells us that Cain was married already at the time of the murder, but the Islamic belief disagrees with that. Nod was East of Eden, or toward the area of Manchuria. Below is a list of the descendents of Cain and their different names by different cultures.

Bible Name	Hebrew	Sumerian	Mesopotamian
Cain	Qayan		
Enoch	Chanock	Anunaki, Anunni	Uanna-Adapa
Irad	Yrad		
Mehujael	Mehujael		
Methushael	Methushael		
Lamech I	Lamech I		
Tubal Cain	Tubal Qayan		Chrysor, Vulcan

21a. **Enoch ben Cain:** Cain's livelihood taken away and his connection to HaShem, Cain began to start his family. Enoch was the first born son. David Rohl tells us that another name for Enoch was Anunnaki. They are pronounced very much the same. *The Book of Jubilee* has Enoch being born around 196 A.T. (after the birth of Adam's son, Seth). David Rohl has Enoch becoming a god rather than just a king (E-no-chee). The *Epic of Gilgamesh* (written well after the Flood of Noah) refers to Inanna, the highest god. (This is not believed in this work to refer to HaShem, but to the first of many false gods). Lilitu / Lilith is referred to in this same epic work who was closely attached to this god, Inanna. This ties Lilith to the line of Cain. The Egyptian text, *Text of Shebitu*, refers to both of them being of the original gods from the early days of creation. Rohl believes that Eridu was Enki or Enochi (Enoch). It is easy to believe that false gods were raised up among Cain's descendents, since HaShem had cut Cain off from any connection to HaShem. The Hebrew history, *Seder Olam*, believes that Enoch introduced idolatry to the world by creating a mud figure. Satan then entered the idol. The Hebrew word is *hukal* which means rebellion. This word is only used 3 times in the Torah/Bible; The 2nd time in Genesis 6 when the men of the heavens married the daughters of men and the 3rd time with Nimrod.

The Epic of Beowulf (lines 110-114) indicates that Grendel was a spawn of Cain. Ancient mythologies attach older gods to Cain (i.e. Osiris of Egyptian mythology). The mythology of Osiris is that he was killed and cut into many pieces by Set (or Seth, possibly the son of Adam). Menes (Manas-tishu, son of Sargon I) mentions Cain as one of his ancestors. Menes calls Cain the son of Ukusi (The Sumerian name for Adam).

Cain built a city and named it after Enoch. The pronunciation of the city is Unuk (Uruk) which was later established after the flood as a Babylonian city. While the flood destroyed much of the civilization, many parts were simply covered in mud and earth slides. Many of the cities simply had to be uncovered after the flood and some of the building structures would already be there. While the flood was a major catastrophe, only life forms were totally decimated, not necessarily all buildings.

Enoch had a son, Irad, and David Rohl believes that Cain built another city called Eridu (Iradu). This later became the place of the Temple of Jupiter, or the Tower of Babylon. Irad became a High Priest of the Cain population.

Adam and Eve had other sons and daughters who worshipped HaShem, as Adam and Eve did. Over the course of years, some of those would have mixed with Cain's descendents and the lines would become blurred, and religious differences would become reality. Cain too had other descendents and it is believed that Cain's descendents were kings of the ancient world; Mehujael, Methushael, and then Lamech I. Tubal Cain, one of Lamech's sons, is believed by John Jackson (circa 1752 A.D.) to have been deified as the god Vulcan by the Phoenicians. This cult was carried across the flood through the wife of Ham who was a descendent of Cain.

21b. **Ancient Kings:** An ancient king list called the *Sumerian King List (SKL)* records a list of kings compiled by post Flood historians. David Rohl does not believe that the pre-flood portion of the list is valid or accurate and this work is inclined to agree with Rohl. The pre-flood list was added to the overall list at a much later date, by Isin writers, *Isin King List* (IKL). Isin priests came across the ancient kings and didn't know what to do with them. Rather than place them in parallel with post-flood kings as probably should have taken place, they simply put them before the flood.

Thorkild Jacobsen was the first to translate the SKL in 1939 from Sumerian. He discovered that the Sumerian numbers for the years of rule were different than our modern number system. Herman Hoeh believed that the symbols were coded instead of actual numbers. Diodorus Siculus (*Book I*) discovered that the years listed in the SKL were lunar years rather than solar years (28000 years should be 28000 / 12. Then it was decided that they used a sexagesimal system. The symbol for 10 in Semitic is the same symbol as the number 60 in Sumerian. The early interpreters were using the Semitic interpretation which means that the numbers were inflated by 6 times. John Jackson discovered that the dates given by Berossus (quoted by Eusebius) were actually in sars (1 sar equals 222 lunar months or 18 years and 6 months).

The importance of this king list is that it is a valid archaeological document outside of the Bible and the Koran that validates the Flood of Noah, something that modern scientists have tried to say is nothing more than a small local flood and not a real world wide catastrophe. The first fragment of the SKL was published in 1906 A.D. It was found in the Library of Nippur during an archaeological dig. Several versions of the SKL were found and they all agree with one another. L. Austine Waddell discovered that the translations differed widely due to the lack of understanding the ancient language and having no dictionary to use. The problem was that different sounds were given to the letters by different interpreters which resulted in the same word being pronounced in different ways and therefore were *perceived* to be different words. One example of this is the word "Gilgamesh". It was translated as Gilgamesh, Gigamesh, Gilgames, Izdubar, and Gishtobar by different translators. Professor Arno Poebel published a better translation in 1914 A.D. A stone bowl, *Udu's Stone Bowl*, was found that had the names of the first 4 kings of Kish on the bowl, validating the SKL/IKL. In 1924, an official list of the IKL were published by Assyriologists including the kings that were put before the Flood. Waddell believed that this publication was corrupt and in 1939, Jacobsen reconstructed the list. It was also discovered that many of the lists in the IKL were contemporary, not sequential as originally believed. Waddell discovered that the list resembled many names in another (and quite separate document) called the *Kish Chronicles* and then yet another list of kings called the *Aryan King List* (AKL) found in India. All of the lists had holes, but by placing the lists together, many of the holes were filled.

The last list to be discussed is the *Paschal Chronicles*. This relates the first Chaldean Kings to giants. Berossus copies Enoch in saying Azazyel as the demon taught men the working of weapons, related to Tubal Cain.

21a. **Cosmology:** At this time, this work draws a logical conclusion from day 4 of creation that the only orbs in the heavens were the earth, the sun, and the second star, called Uranus (see section 11). The Hebrew history believes that during the time of Enoch, a huge flood engulfed a third of the world. Immanuel Velikovsky gives evidence that ancient mythologies were the eyewitness accounts of men of the events going on in the heavens. Since they had no telescopes, the ancients were only able to report what could be seen with the naked eye.

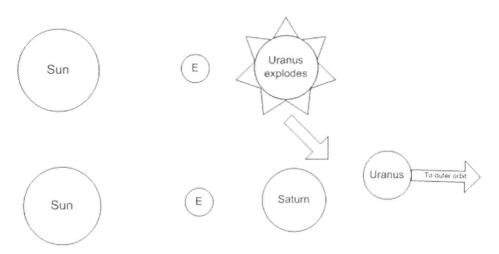

With the breaking off of Cain from HaShem, men from his line began to see the orbs in the sky as gods. Uranus, strangely is the first god in most ancient civilizations, even though the sun is bigger. This is due to the fact that Uranus was closer to the earth and *appeared to be larger*. The ancients knew about the rings of Saturn, and the moons of Jupiter and Mars, which gives a strong indication that they could *see these orbs*. Greek mythology says that Uranus and Gaia (earth) were the first gods. They gave birth to Cyclops and Titans, large giants that roamed the earth at this time.

A huge flood in the time of Enoch gives support to a cosmological event that affected the earth due to the close proximity of the planets. Around this time, Uranus *disappeared* and Saturn became the new ruling deity of the heavens. Kronos / Saturn too began to destroy small planets that came from it, until Jupiter, a larger planet escaped (supposedly hidden by Gaia). It has been known for many years that Uranus, Saturn, and Jupiter give off more heat than they absorb from the sun. The theory of Velikovsky, De Grazia, and this work is that Uranus (a star rather than a planet) exploded and the explosion caused a now much smaller Uranus to be pushed out to its current orbit, out of the eyesight range of the inhabitants of earth, thus *appearing to have been destroyed by Saturn*. The ancients also knew about the moons of Saturn, orbs that cannot be seen by the naked eye in our current solar system cosmology. Velikovsky and De Grazia believe that our current moon came into existence at this time.

At this time, Saturn did not appear to have rings around it, as testified later when Zeus / Jupiter chained Saturn. If Jupiter was created at this time, the planet was further out than Saturn, thus explaining why Saturn became the main god for many centuries, while Jupiter remained as a hidden son of Saturn. The *"Sibylline Oracles"* report that Jupiter appeared during the fight between Saturn and Uranus. Saturn is related to water catastrophes through history and this would explain the flooding taking place on earth during their close encounter with the earth during the struggle in the solar system.

The fact that the ancients knew about all the planets of our solar system and their moons well before the invention of the telescope is evidence that modern day evolutionists cannot explain. According to the evolution theory, our solar system hasn't changed in millions of years and yet, the ancient mythologies and their *accuracy about our solar system planets and moons* indicates that the ancient people were able to view the planets at some point.

22. **Bereshit / Genesis 5: Seth ben Adam:** The year is 130 A.T. or 3834 B.C. Most Christians jump to the conclusion that Seth is the 3rd son of Adam. There is no evidence in the Bible that this is true. Cain gave evidence that there were other people on the earth during his last conversation with HaShem saying how those people would hunt him to hurt him. Seth was a *replacement* for Abel. The birth of Seth definitely took place after the murder of Abel, but it is not known when. Seth was called out by HaShem in the Torah due to his ancestry over the Messiah many thousands of years later. *The Book of Jubilees* has Seth being born 32 years after Abel's death, but the opinion given here is that this book is not very accurate in giving a timeline.

The Book of Adam and Eve is believed to have been written by Seth. An excerpt of the book tells how Satan came to Genun and showed him how to make musical instruments, alcohol, colored dyes for clothing and tattoos for the body. *The Book of Enoch* agrees that it was Satan (Azael) whom taught men how to make weapons and cosmetics. Enoch 97 says that colleges of witchcraft were formed to give certificates of graduation. The Gezer version of the Book of Enoch says that Enoch declared war on the sons of Cain and caused the death of many. Enoch (of Seth's line) had a son, Methushelah, who continued to war against the demons and evil factions of the world. Methushelah was the grandfather of Noah.

Descendents of Seth are considered the ancestors of Yeshua direct to Adam. Julius Africanus, Demetrius, Hippolytus of Rome, Hippolytus of Thebes, Eusebius, and David Rohl all use the Septuagint version of the Bible for their dates. The Samarian version was proven to be false by John Jackson (circa 1752 A.D.), *"Chronological Antiquities"*. According to the Samaritan version, Yared, Methushelah, and Lamech all died the same year. James Ussher (translator of the King James Version of the Bible) and this work both rely on the Masoretic version for the dates. James Ussher also wrote a concise history of the Bible with relation to world history. Unfortunately, in the 1600's he did not have full access to all the documents that are now available, as well as to the archaeology of the last 400 years, so many of his dates are flawed. The *Revised History of the Ancient World* uses the example set by James Ussher in using numbered paragraphs instead of page numbers for the referenced index.

Hebrew historians show that cavemen (mal-nutritional men and women) lived during the time of the early patriarchs. They indicate that the demonic influences and possession of men gave them the appearance of cavemen and ape like men (Neanderthal). It might be mentioned that the extended ages of men, would also apply to animals. Reptiles and Amphibians grow their entire life, so applying a 900 year growth to many of the cold blooded animals would result in huge sizes, i.e. dinosaurs. Since men did not eat meat, these large creatures had little to fear from men.

The following chart are the years of birth for the pre-flood patriarchs.

Mas = Masoretic and Revised A.T.; Sam = Samaritan; LXX = Septuagint; Jos = Josephus; J.U. = James Ussher (B.C.); Rohl = David Rohl B.C.; Rev B.C. = Revised B.C.

Name	Mas	Sam	LXX	Jos	J.U.	Rohl	Rev B.C.
Adam	1	1	1	1	4004	5375	3963
Seth ben Adam	130	130	230	230	3874	5155	3834
Enos ben Seth	235	235	435	435	3769	4940	3729
Kenan ben Enos	325	325	625	625	3679	4750	3639

Mehalalel ben Kenan	395	395	795	795	3609	4580	3569
Yared ben Mehalalel	460	460	960	960	3544	4418	3504
Enoch ben Yared	622	522	1122	1122	3382	4253	3342
Methushelah	687	587	1287	1287	3317	4088	3277
Lamech II	874	654	1474	1474	3130	3901	3090
Noah	1056	707	1662	1656	2948	3713	2908
Shem	1558	1209	2164	2156	2446	3213	2406
Flood of Noah	1656	1307	2262	2256	2349	3113	2308

Disparity of Bible Versions: M.T. = Masoretic Text Dating; S.T. = Syrian Text Dating; LXX = Septuagint

Patriarch	Age at time of son's birth			Total Years lived		
	M.T. A.T.	S.T. A.M.	LXX A.M.	M.T. A.T.	S.T. A.M.	LXX A.M.
Adam	130	130	230	930	930	930
Seth	105	105	205	912	912	912
Enos ben Seth	90	90	190	905	905	905
Kenan ben Enos	70	70	170	910	910	910
Mehalalel	65	65	165	895	895	895
Yared	162	62	162	962	847	962

Patriarch	Age at time of son's birth			Total Years lived		
	M.T. A.T.	S.T. A.M.	LXX A.M.	M.T. A.T.	S.T. A.M.	LXX A.M.
Enoch ben Yared	65	65	165	365	365	365
Methushulah	187	67	187	969	847	969
Lamech II	182	53	188	777	653	753
Noah	600	600	600	930		
Methush. at flood	969	720	975			
Flood	1656	1307	2262			

22a. **Bereshit / Genesis 6:4: Yared ben Mehalalel:** The years are between 460 A.T. and 622 A.T. *Yared* means to descend. It was during the days of Yared that the divine beings began to mate with the daughters of men. This resulted in a new kind of man, Nephilim. Some of these were superhuman, while others were sub human, the cavemen of the Hebrew history. These unholy creatures were base in nature. Since Enoch is not included the verse, these unholy unions took place in the early days of Yared before his son, Enoch was born. Job refers to the *sons of God* being angels, and thus refutes the idea of the divine beings being humans.

Panodorus wrote around 500 A.D. that Egregori / Nephilim descended around the year 1000 A.T. (he used the LXX version of the Bible) which would translate to around 500 A.T. in the Masoretic version. Syncellus agrees with Panodorus. The Haggadah reports that 200 angels descended to earth to mate with the daughters. *The Book of Enoch* agrees with that number. These Nephilim taught women the arts of medicine and herbs, *witchcraft*. The leader, Shemhazai had 2 sons, Hiwwa and Hiyya. The pronunciation of these two is the same as is found in *The Epic of Gilgamesh.*

They were the gods that Gilgamesh was trying to destroy. Gilgamesh was one of the early kinds, descendents of Nimrod after the flood.

22b. Enoch ben Yared: The Hebrew histories believe he was a ruler in his own right over the *righteous* of the earth for 243 years. He is credited with 2 books, but due to the tampering of early Christians, his books were excluded from the Bible. According to the Haggadah, he died the same day he was born, 365 years old. Josephus does not believe that Enoch was a good man. According to the Book of Enoch, Enoch battled against many giants, titans, and demons. This supports the *mythology* of Saturn who gave birth to titans and giants (and possibly to Nephilim). This comparison is not intended to give credibility to the mythologies as *gods*, but simply to show that mythology and the Bible somehow coincide to validate the Bible stories by eyewitness accounts outside of the Biblical narrative.

The Nephilim (part angel) went to Enoch for help, but HaShem told them that it was the duty of angels to intercede for humans, not the other way around. *The Book of Giants (Dead Sea Scrolls)* says that the Nephilim were monsters. Men declared war on the giants and the *Book of Baruch* says that over 400,000 giants were killed in the Flood of Noah. *The Pearl of Great Price of Moses* says that the giants knew that Noah would bring the flood and sought to end his life before he could finish the ark. Enoch was taken to heaven without experiencing death, which gives rise to the belief that he *might* be one of the two witnesses of *Revelation* in the final days of the Wrath of HaShem.

22c. Methushelah: He is the grandfather of Noah and he lived the longest on earth, 969 years. *The Book of Enoch* gives Enoch's age as 165 when Methushelah was born, but the Masoretic text gives us Enoch's age at 65. The Haggadah indicates that Methushelah had a sword with the ineffable name of HaShem on it that allowed him to kill demons with the sword. During his time, before Lamech was born, a huge famine killed a large number of people on the earth.

22d. Noah: He was called Menachem by Lamech. Noah means rest or comfort and might be a name given to him by Moses when the Pentateuch was written rather than his real name. The date of his birth, Iyyar 17, 1056 A.T. is based on the exact day he entered the ark, when he was exactly 600 years old. His Greek name was Xisuthrus and Gilgamesh met with Noah and called him Utnapishtin. The *Dead Sea Scrolls (Q534-536)* says he was born at night, 7 pounds and 3 ounces, more archaeological evidence of Biblical narratives outside of the Bible.

22e. **Sons of Noah:** Noah married according to the Hebrew chronology two years before his 500th birthday. His first son was born on his 500th birth year. The sons are not listed in order of birth, but by order of importance. In order of birth, Japheth was born in 1556 A.T., Shem in 1558 A.T., and Ham, the last, sometime after Shem but time unknown. Shem's birth is known exactly by calculations of the birth of his son, Arpachshad 2 years after the flood. Shem was 100 years old at the time of Arpachshad's birth. *The Book of Jubilee* places Japheth's birth in 1207 A.M. (LXX) and Julius Africanus places the birth in 2162 A.Ad. (A.Ad. dating form referenced from the year of Adam's birth but also based on the LXX). The date from Jubilee is obviously wrong and all future dates from this reference are to be taken as error prone, but listed for the curiosity of the reader.

CHAPTER 5

AGE OF NOAH

23. **Bereshit / Genesis 6:1-13:** HaShem sees that men have become corrupt, but the main reason for HaShem's descent is that the daughters of men have accepted divine beings and begat monsters (6:2) and heroes of renown (6:4) which lead to a huge increase in violence around the earth. This violence will be duplicated in the *end of days* (Matthew 24:37-38) (during the last 50 years of the 6000 year period of history). The Haggadah reports that Naamah bar (daughter) of Lamech I ben Cain introduced women to bestiality. Naamah had sex with a demon and begat Asmodeus. Islamic tradition says that Naamah begat offspring by two angels/djinn; Azael and Aza. The Muslim tradition equates the Nephilim angels with the djinn who were able to mate with daughters of men.

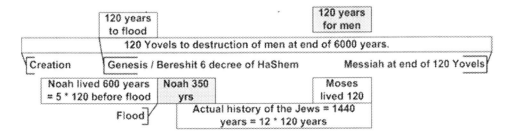

He descends and designates 120 years for men. Numbers have huge meanings in the Torah, but the meanings have to be carefully derived from context. In this case, 120 has many connections in the Torah. In this verse, it is taken to predict the Flood of Noah in 120 years. The year of this descent is 1536 A.T./2428 B.C.

The 120 also applies to the number of Yovels in a 6000 year history (6000 / 50 years per yovel = 120 Yovels). And finally, the context of this verse could apply to the number of years of a man's lifetime. This last one is questionable as most of the patriarchs lived well beyond 120 years shortly after the flood. It is interesting to note that Moses died at exactly 120 years of age. The revised history of the Jews takes 1440 years, which is 12 * 120.

23a. Announcement of Flood: The Haggadah says that the announcement came to Noah via the angel Uriel. Azazyel was put in chains by Raphael until Judgment Day. HaShem's descent to deal with the wickedness of mankind is 4th descent and by definition of this work, issues in a new age which has been referred to as the Age of Noah. Dispensational theories link the actual flood to the break in dispensations, but this work ties the change to the *descent* of HaShem, which took place earlier than the flood by 120 years, to prepare Noah to prepare for the Flood.

23b. Ark: The length of the ark was like 2 football fields. Having discussed the significance of numbers, the description of the ark has symbolic meaning, but deciphering that meaning can lead to confusion rather than illumination.

Modern Biblical theologians surmise that the ark was a *sewn boat*, meaning it was built by building the sides and then sewing them together. This has the advantage of being capable of being built by few men and by primitive tools, *"Biblical Archaeological Review Vol 31 No 3"*. The shape of the ark was more like a barge with huge rocks at the bottom to keep the barge from tipping over. Even if it was submerged for a short time, it would immediately float to the top. On April 27, 2010 A.D. a group of Chinese and Turkish explorers believe they found the ark on Mount Ararat in Eastern Turkey. Yeung Wing-Cheung was the leader of the archaeological group.

23c. Figurative Language of the Ark: This work recognizes that not only is HaShem a God of full disclosure, but that some of His disclosure comes in the form of *archetypes or types* meaning that events, people, and things are representative of things to come. In this case, it is believed by this work that the ark is a *type of Messiah*. The large door in the side represents the spear piercing the side of Yeshua while He hung on the cross.

It was the spilling of this blood that seeped into the Holy cup buried in a cave beneath where He was crucified that was the payment for our sins. The ark was *finished* in the 600th year of Noah, and the salvation of Yeshua will take place in the 6000th year of the history of the world. It was started 120 years before it was finished, and the salvation work of HaShem started 120 Yovels before the work was finished. The window at the top guarantees that an opening to HaShem will always exist.

24. **Bereshit / Genesis 7**: **The Flood:** Noah is ordered to go into the Ark. This was 7 days before the flood started, or Iyyar 10, 1656 A.T. 595840 D.T. / April 26, 2308 B.C. 878197 J.D. The Hebrew chronology places it in the same year. Julius Africanus places this event in the year 2262 A.M. (Anno Mundi or Year of the World based on the LXX version). Hippolytus of Rome, Hippolytus of Thebes, and Eusebius place this event in 2242 A.M. Noah was 600 years old. Methushelah died just a few days before the flood according to the Jewish Chronology and was 969 years old. The Hebrew chronology places this event in the 2nd month which is Cheshvan. Methushelah died on the 11th of Cheshvan by their chronology. Flavius Josephus (of 100 A.D.) estimates a date of October 20, 2106 A.M. using the Hebrew chronology of that time which had already established Tishrei as the 1st month of the year. Dr. Floyd Nolan Jones places the year in 2348 B.C. differing from this revised date by 40 years. Frank Klassen places the flood in the year 2319 B.C. and Jack Finegan in the year 2104 B.C.

The denial of the flood having taken place by modern historians is mostly based on their prejudice against believing in HaShem and the Jews. The flood story permeates historical records even into modern Russia. The most widely known reference to the flood was in the *Epic of Gilgamesh*, but modern historians reduced this document to nothing but mere myth. According to the epic, Noah lived in Shuruppak when the flood occurred. The Chaldean version of the flood has it starting on the 15th day of the 2nd month, (the spring of the year). The following is a non-Biblical record of the flood by the Greek historian Berossus. The Islamic version is exactly like the Hebrew version except the name of the mountain where Noah's ark first landed: Al-Judi. The Russian version is the same except that they have Noah's wife being influenced by Satan.

Berossus is quoted by Eusebius of Caesaria (a documented and recorded historian of ancient times) about the flood:

"When Otiartes died, his son Xisuthrus became king, for 18 sars. In his reign, the great flood occurred. This is how the story is told. Cronus (whom they call the father of Zeus, while others call him Chronus ["time"]) approached him in his sleep, and said that on the 15th day of the month of Daesius the human race would be destroyed by a flood. Cronus ordered him to bury the beginnings, the middles and the ends of all writings in Heliopolis, the city of the Sippareni(ancient city of Shuruppak)*; to build a boat and embark on it with his close friends; to load the boat with food and drink, and to put on board every kind of bird and four-footed creature; and then, when all the preparations were complete, to sail away. When he asked where he should sail, Cronus replied, "To the gods, to pray that good things may happen to men." Xisuthrus did as he had been told. He built a boat which was 15 stades long and 2 stades wide. After completing everything as instructed, he sent his wife, his children and his close friends onto the boat.*

When the flood had come, and soon afterwards stopped, Xisuthrus sent out some of the birds. But they could not find any food or anywhere to rest, and so they returned to the boat. A few days later, Xisuthrus sent out the birds again, and this time they returned to the boat with mud on their feet. The third time that he sent out the birds, they no longer returned to the boat. Xisuthrus realized that some land had appeared. He removed part of the sides of the boat, and saw that it had come to rest on a mountain. He disembarked with his wife and daughter and the helmsman, and kissed the ground. After he had set up an altar and had sacrificed to the gods, he disappeared from sight, along with the others who had left the boat with him. When Xisuthrus and his companions did not return, the remainder of those who were on the boat disembarked andsearched for himand called out his name. They could not see Xisuthrus anywhere, but a voice came out of the sky telling them that they should honour the gods, and that Xisuthrus had gone to live with the gods, because of the honour he showed them; his wife, his daughter and the helmsman had received the same reward. The voice told them to return to Babylon; they were destined to dig up the writings which had been hidden in the city of the Sippareni, and distribute them amongst men. They were told that they were now in the land of Armenia.

When they heard all of this, they sacrificed to the gods and went by foot to Babylon. A small part of the boat, which came to rest in Armenia, can still be found in the mountains of the Cordyaei in Armenia. Some people scrape off the asphalt, which covers the boat, and use it to ward off diseases, like an amulet. When they arrived back in Babylon, they dug up the writings in the city of the Sippareni. They founded many cities, and re-founded Babylon, constructing many temples."

The document above is a Greek document which contradicts modern historians in claiming that the Noahic Flood was merely a local area flood. This flood covered the entire earth. Immanuel Velikovsky has noted that the lava flows (which is usually along a magnetic path on earth) have shown that they have not always flowed toward what we call north now. The flood was a *catastrophic* event with waters breaking up the land masses in huge earthquakes. The population didn't just drown. They were crushed and killed in massive events and falling waters.

24a. **Cosmological Forces of the Flood**: This revised work wishes it to be known that the supernatural influence of HaShem is heavily at play in this flood, but that being said, the external and non-supernatural explanation is that Khima (Saturn or Kronos) and Jupiter were at war in the heavens. Neptune seems to have been involved as well. The Haggadah reports that Saturn lit the sky up for 7 days during the week of the 10th of Iyyar until the 17th, the day that Noah entered the ark (on his 600th birthday). The Book of Job confirms that the star that lit the skies was Khima (Saturn). The Talmud says that Jupiter pushed Saturn out of visual sight. The sky was lit up both day and night, giving Noah and his family a full week of light to complete the loading of the ark with the different species.

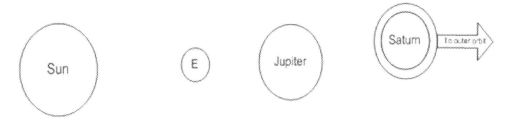

The mythological story is that Jupiter defeated Saturn and wrapped Saturn in chains. The ancient witnesses to this cosmological event were able to see the *rings/chains* of Saturn with their eyes, something that cannot be done to this day without a telescope. Saturn is then pushed out into its current orbit much the way Uranus was in the Saturn Uranus conflict. Egyptian mythology has Osiris being drowned on the 17th day of their 2nd month. Diodorus Siculus says that Osiris was the *son of Saturn, not Saturn himself.* The *Fast of Tammuz* takes place on this day, 17th. *The Epic of Marduk (Jupiter)* indicates that Jupiter was responsible for the flood. The Greek legends have Pluto (Hades) being pushed out into its current orbit. Again, the question is how did the ancients know about these cosmological orbs unless they had seen them first hand? Equally astonishing is that they knew about Pluto, Uranus, Neptune, and Saturn all planets in the furthest parts of our solar system and yet no mention of Venus has been made as of yet. The earth was flipped and pushed around by the close interactions of the larger planets. It was after this that Jupiter became the leading god in most civilizations (Norse, Egyptian, Greek, Chinese, India, and Phoenicia). After the flood, in the Torah, Shem ben Noah became known as Melchitzedek which is commonly translated as the King of Peace, but Tzedek also means Jupiter. Shem became known as the King of Jupiter. This is rejected by modern Christian theologians because the idea that Shem worshipped other gods is abhorrent, but this name in no way reflects Shem's devotion or lack thereof to HaShem. Shem was a powerful king of his time and he would be bound to have other names just as Noah did.

The Orphic Tradition has Jupiter growing up in Dictyan caves near Lato. When he grew up, he freed his brothers and sisters from captivity and waged war on Kronos/Saturn. The Hekadoncheries and the Cyclopes are released from their prison in Tartarus and they join forces with Jupiter. Atlas commanded the Titans. The war lasted 10 years. Zeus then takes Hera, his sister, as his wife. Inachus became king of the Argives at this time when Zeus wins the battle and Kronos is exiled to Elysia and rules over Sicily and Italy. This version of Jupiter is not connected to the mythology of the events of the flood as they take place many years later. Inachus lives many years after the flood.

24b. **Population of the Ark:** The biggest mistake of modern historians is in believing that every modern species had to be aboard the ark. Thanks to Darwin's Theory of Natural Selection, this isn't true. Two of each species had to be aboard, but not two of each variation of each species. For instance, there only needed to be 2 fox. Red Fox, gray fox, other varieties would develop out of these two original fox based on Darwin's Theory. This greatly reduces the number of animals on the ark. The sea creatures did not need to be there, which makes for an even shorter list of species on the ark. The water tables were lower before the flood, so that land masses were connected, allowing all manners of creatures to appear to Noah to be loaded. In this, the modern historian scoffs, but that's because they deny the supernatural influence of HaShem in this process. Denying HaShem's influence will greatly limit the ability to understand what happened.

There were 8 people aboard the ark and only 8. This brings into question the giants who lived during the time of Joshua. There are some Hebrew sources that indicates that giants clung to the ark for the duration of the flood. Others believe that Ham's wife not only carried the Cushite gene (black skin) but also the giant gene so that her grandchildren and descendents would have that gene and carry it on. The solid answer just isn't there. Darwin's theory just doesn't hold for the idea of one generation being black by adaptation. Cush was a son of Ham and he was black, while his father was white. Either Ham's wife was black, or she carried the black gene to give forth a black baby. Since they were on the ark for a year and 10 days, it is unlikely that she was pregnant on the ark itself and Cush was not her firstborn. None of the grandsons of Noah were born until after they had disembarked from the ark. There just isn't a solid answer for the giants, but they most certainly did live during the time of Joshua.

24c. **Bereshit/Genesis 8-9: Covenant of Noah:** This was the result of Noah's offering to HaShem after they landed, on the Tsivan 1st feast, later described in the Law of Moses, as the *Feast of Weeks*. Modern theologians and Christians believe that the promises to Adam and Eve were the first covenant, but this isn't true. A covenant from HaShem is always accompanied by a sign. In Noah's case, the rainbow was the sign of the covenant. Noah became a farmer and wine maker. Noah lived after the flood for 350 years (7 more Yovels). He lived for 950 years, a long time after the 120 year limit imposed by Hashem 120 years earlier. He was the last man to live over 900 years. The 8 spoke 1 language, which this revised version believes is Hebrew. The orthodox Hebrew view is that the first language was Hebrew as well. Bereshit / Genesis 9:1 says that HaShem blessed Noah *and his sons.* The blessing indicates that the beasts of the earth will dread humans. This was the first time that meat was given to eat. Before the flood, mankind was vegetarian.

24d. **Height of the Flood:** Modern archaeologists and historians would wish to infer that this flood was a local flood to the valley of Mesopotamia. There are two levels in the earth's crust that indicate where the world was *covered in water completely.* The first contained no fossil structures (and thus is given an age of 500 million years ago by evolution theorists). The second contained not only sea fossils but that of many creatures as well. This level covered the entire world. The Torah says that the waters covered the highest mountains by *fifteen cubits*. The Torah says that the only life left was on the ark, which rules out the giants living through the flood.

24e. **Curse of Canaan:** Canaan was the son of Ham. When Ham uncovered his father's nakedness, Noah cursed Canaan. He could not curse Ham because Ham had been blessed by HaShem. When the lands were divided up, Canaan got the land that would belong to the Israelites, under Abraham. This curse caused his enslavement to Abraham's descendents many years later. Since Canaan was the 4th son of Ham, this event of Noah's drunkenness must have taken place at *least* 5 to 6 years after the ark landed on Ararat and likely it took place up to 25 years after the ark landed as Canaan was a young man by then. One of the reasons that Canaan might have been chosen to be cursed was that he had stolen the land of Canaan after it was allotted to someone else. There are some Hebrew sources that indicate that the action taken by Ham was more than just uncovering Noah's nakedness and that some violation took place.

25. **Bereshit / Genesis 10-11: Generations of Noah:** There is no record that any of the wives were pregnant on the ark or got pregnant on the ark. The three wives got pregnant after the ark. Shem's wife brought forth Shem's first son, Arpachshad, in Shem's 100th year, 2 years after the flood.

The year is 1658 A.T. / 2306 B.C. Julius Africanus places Arpachshad's birth in 2262 A.M. (LXX). *The Book of Jubilee* gives him a birth year of 1429 A.M. The Jewish chronology interprets this to be 2 years after the start of the flood, so the year after it was over, he was born. Luke 3:36 places Cainan as the son of Arpachshad and this is confirmed by the LXX and the *Book of Jubilees*. He is not mentioned in the lists of Josephus, the Targum, the Masoretic list of Shem's descendents, and the Samaritan text. James Ussher does not believe Canaan should be in the list of Shem's descendents. The original version of Luke, by Beza, does not include Cainan. Dr. Floyd Nolan Jones indicates that this Cainan is the son of Ham, adopted by Arpachshad when Arpachshad married the widow of Ham. This revised version believes that if this is so, Cainan would be the father of Selah. Another problem with this is that this revised believes that due to the legends and extra-Biblical records, that Ham lived a long time. This revised version believes that somewhere along the way, someone decided to add Canaan to Shem's line without justification.

25a. **Japheth and Ham:** This revised version believes that the three wives of the sons of Noah got pregnant the same year, thus giving birth to their firstborn the same year as Arpachshad. Cush of Ham's line (the first black man) and Gomer of Japheth's line (white) were both born around the same time as Arpachshad, although nothing exact is given in the Torah. Chapter 10 of Bereshit and Genesis gives the generations of Noah and time passes between chapter 10 and 11.

By the end of 10 years, there would be enough people to build small towns and cities, which all 3 sons did. The wild animals were not yet a threat, and diseases had not yet started to spread. Except for war, there was nothing to cause the death of the population which grew logarithmically. War did not take place for many years.

Postdiluvian Patriarchs; MT = Masoretic Text (version used by conventional Hebrew chronology); LXX = Septuagint; LXX Eus. = LXX according to Eusebius; ST = Samaritan Text; JUB = Book of Jubilee; JU = James Ussher; DR = David Rohl's revised dates; LR =Lyle Revised dates. This revised reconstruction follows the years for the MT (A.T.), but offers different Gregorian years than James Ussher or Rohl's revised dates. Table is for births, not dates of rule. Shem would be the ruler all the way through to Abraham as Melchitzedek. The Jewish time for Abraham's birth is 1948 A.M. from the Masoretic Text but follows the M.T.

A.T. otherwise.

Patriarch	M.T. A.T.	LXX A.M.	LXX Eus	S.T. A.M.	Jub A.M.	J.U. B.C.	D.R. B.C.	Rev B.C.
Arpachshad	1658	2264	2264	1309	1429	2346	3011	2306
Canaan / Kenan		2399	Only LXX version. Eusebius excludes					
Shelah	1693	2529	2399	1444	1432	2311	2746	2271
Eber	1723	2659	2529	1574	1499	2281	2616	2241
Peleg	1757	2793	2663	1708	1567	2247	2482	2207
Reu	1787	2923	2793	1838	1628	2217	2352	2177
Serug	1819	3055	2928	1970	1687	2185	2222	2145
Nahor I	1849	3185	3058	2100	1800	2155	2090	2115
Terah	1878	3264	3137	2179	1806	2126	1970	2086
Abraham	2008	3202	3184		1876	1996		1956

Breakout of patriarchs after the flood: MT = Masoretic / Hebrew Text; ST = Samaritan Text; LXX = Septuagint.

Patriarch	Age at time of son's birth			Total Years lived		
	M.T. A.T.	S.T. A.M.	LXX A.M.	M.T. A.T.	S.T. A.M.	LXX A.M.
After Flood	2	2	2			
Arpachshad	35	135	135	435	438	538
Canaan / Kenan			130	Not applicable		
Shelah	30	130	130	433	433	433
Eber	34	134	134	464	404	404
Peleg	30	130	130	239	239	239
Reu	32	132	132	239	239	239
Serug	30	130	130	230	230	230
Nahor I	29	79	79	148	148	208
Terah	70	70	70	205	145	204
Flood to Abram	292	942	942			
Kenan included			1072			

The following are the leading rulers of the new world and their alternate names in different areas of the world.

Biblical	Greek	Mesopotamia	Sumerian	Egyptian
Ham	Her	Enki	Utu	Hor or Har
Cush	Hermes	Bel / Baal	Meskiagkasher	Aethiops
Nimrod	Bachus / Ninus	Marduk / Asar	Enmekar	Asar or Osiris
	Dionysius	Tammuz	Tammuz	Osiris resurrected

26. Civilization: Nimrod wasn't just a king. His title was *patesi* which means priest king. Nimrod was the ruler of the world and the new ruler of a new religious order that no longer wished to abide by the God of Noah. The Bible indicates that he was considered a *hero*, but the actual Hebrew word used for him means *rebel*. The religion of Noah was followed by his three sons, but not the grandsons. Polytheism didn't formulate again until just before the Tower of Babel. Jupiter worship started anew, but the worship of the other orbs as gods didn't take place for a while. Melchitzedek was a priest of the *Most High God*, the God of Noah. Nimrod was deified by Semiramis his wife after Nimrod died to maintain her rule over the people. Rev Hislop believes that she did this to hide the fact that she had a child by her son but she claimed the baby was the reincarnated Nimrod. She was the first known female ruler and she ruled over most of Assyria, including Nineveh. She wasn't able to gain control over Babel, ruled by Nimrod's son after Nimrod's death. She was able to rule over Nineveh for many years, long enough to start wars against India and Phoenicia.

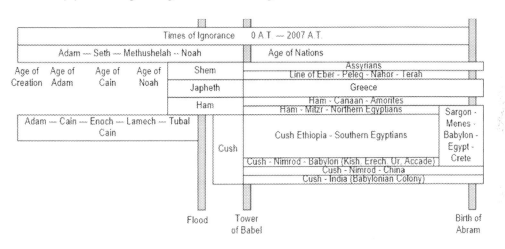

26a. **First Cities**: Nimrod is the son of Cush and his name is mentioned as being one of the early leaders of the new civilization, but from an archaeological standpoint, Cush / Kish (both are spelled the same in the ancient Sumerian language), was the true progenitor of the race. Cush built Kish (Cush) (which location wise was a mere half day's ride from the ancient city of Babel so that they are one and same between the Bible and archaeological records. The king lists of Mesopotamia already mentioned earlier, SKL and IKL, both mention the kings of Kish as the first kings after the flood. Kish is mentioned before Erech (Uruk). David Rohl and L.Austine Waddell both believe that Kish and Erech existed side by side as the first 2 kingdoms of the world and this revised version agrees. Cush, not Nimrod, was the first true ruler of both. Berossus agrees with the Bible/ Torah in citing that Babel was the first true center of the newly populated earth. He indicates that the first several rulers of Babel were black men. The Torah indicates several large centers that were under Nimrod's rule; Akkad (Accad) and Calneh (probably the earliest city of Carchemish or City of Shem – "Car-Shem"). Rabbi W.F. Albright believes the modern city of Kullani is the same city. Amos 6:2 and Isaiah 10:9 both mention Calno as being the same as Carchemish. Calno is close to Hamath and Gath of the Philistines. Nineveh was an Assyrian center. Asshur was founded by Asshur, son of Shem. There were 2 branches of Assyrians as will be attested to later. Rehoboth-Ur or just simply Ur. These are all listed under Nimrod, but their development took many years between them.

Bible Name	Archaeological Name	Bible Name	Archaeological Name
Babel	Bab-ilu, Kish, Babylon	Accad	Akkad, Agade
Erech	Uruk, Unuk	Ur	Ur, Uri City

Never does the Bible infer that Nimrod *built the early cities of Mesopotamia*. Rather the Torah says that he *ruled over them*. His father Cush was the builder and the first ruler of these cities. More than 35 small pyramids (precursors to Egypt's magnificent wonders) were built in the Sudan area of Kish, between Egypt and Chaldea. Cush colonized the Sudan area and then, leaving Nimrod to rule over the Mesopotamia area, he built ships and colonized Ethiopia, in East Africa, India, and China. The *Bamboo Annals* of China indicates that a man named Koush (black man) was the absolute first ruler in China.

26b. **Noah's cities:** Ron Wyatt (an amateur archaeologist from the Seventh Day Adventist Church) believes that Noah built the first true village before all others. It is little known due to its small size and location; *Village of Eight*. Due to his lack of credentials, many archaeologists doubt his findings.

Shem is the chosen ancestral line that leads to the birth of the Messiah. Eusebius says that Shem's descendants inhabited Mesopotamia and Assyria. Elam and Aram were very close to the land of Canaan. Elam was the gave birth to the Persians and Elymaeans. Eusebius indicates that Nineveh was built by Asshur and was later renamed Ninus. Shem follows the God of his father, Noah. Assyria's name came from Asher ben Shem but not for many years later. The Sumerian name for Mars is Azar or Ashar, but Mars is not yet a planet in its current orbit. Like Venus, Mars has an orbit of that of a comet.

Diodorus Siculus writes that the Assyrians have very few written records. Nimrod ruled over Assyria as well as Babel and Uruk. His son, by Semiramis, Ninyas, ruled over Nineveh after him but he co-ruled with his mother, Semiramis. This lineage continued over Assyria until Sardanapallus.

From Eusebius concerning the Assyrians of Shem:

"They say that the sons of Shem were Elam, Asshur, Arphaxad, Aram and Lud. Elam was the ancestor of the Elymaeans, the most ancient tribe of the Persians, who founded the city of Elymais. Asshur was the ancestor of the Assyrians; he founded the city of Nineveh, which was later restored by Ninus the king of the Assyrians, who renamed it Ninus after his own name. Arphaxad was the ancestor of the Arphaxaeans, who were also called Chaldaeans. Aram was the ancestor of the Aramaeans, who were also called Syrians. Lud was the ancestor of the Lydians. Arphaxad was the father of Shelah, and Shelah was the father of Eber, from whom the name and nation of the Hebrews (Ebrews) was derived. The sixth in succession from Eber was Abraham, the patriarch of the Jewish nation, in the tenth generation after the flood. That is sufficient to show in brief the close relationship between the Hebrews and the Chaldaeans and Assyrians. Therefore it is fitting after [the Assyrians] to start on the chronology of the Hebrews."

27. **First Babylonian Empire:** Cush and Nimrod were co-rulers in that Cush left the rule to Nimrod while he went around the world and colonized the lands farther away. The two of them together ruled the entire world, including early Greece. *Bamboo Annals* of China tells us that Cush and Nimrod were co-rulers even over China. Lagash is typically dated much later, but comparing the names of the SKL, there were some very early coincidences of names. Castor relates Belus of the Assyrians to Cush. Castor says that Cush assisted Jupiter in his battles against the Titans (giants that have now re-populated the earth as well). The legends of Heracles are mentioned in aiding the Assyrians. Isaiah (46:1) mentions Bel (another name for Cush). *"Bel stoops down, Nebo stoops."* Nebo is Nimrod and is considered to be the first *false prophet.* Cush is called Hermes (*son of Hor – Hor being another name for Ham*).

Revised list of early Babylonian Empire

Ruler	A.T. / B.C.	Notes
Noah	1658 / 2306	
Ham, Kham, Hor, Har	1668 / 2296	Shem in Assyria
Cush, Kish,	1673 / 2291	Arpachshad in Assyria
Nimrod, Nimmirud	1678 / 2286	
Tammuz	1716 / 2248	Ninyas ben Nimrod in Nineveh
Uziwatar	1724 / 2240	
Babum	1730 / 2234	
Pa-Annum	1740 / 2224	
Kalibum	1751 / 2213	
Lugal-banda	1754 / 2210	
Gilgamesh	1760 / 2204	Hoang Ti of China
Tower of Babel Falls		
Uruash	1764 / 2200	
Mukh, Etana the Shepherd		Terah born
Bagu, Baussa		
Enishib, Ennun-nad		
Medi of Kish		

Early kings of Kish: Waddell and other interpreters

Kish Chronicle	Aryan King List	Sumerian King List	Other	Years
Ukusi	Iksh-vaku, Sakko, Indra	Gishur	Cush	30
Azag, Ama, Bakus	Ayus, Bikukshi	Azag	Nimrod	12
Azag at Kish		Azag	Nimrod	64
Naksha an-enuzu	Nahusha, Aya, Janak	Nangis-lisma	Lugalbanda	25
Sagaga	Yayati or Iapat (Japheth)	Yayati		6
Zimugun, Ginmugun	Janamejaya, Puru, Gina	Dumuzi, Janame	Tammuz	30
Uziwitar	Wishtara	Wishtara		6
Mutin	Matinara	Ma, Babum		11
Imuashshu	Vishamsu	Piash-enzu		11
Nailiana	Ilina, Anila	Nashu		3

Everyone in the very early years of development spoke the same language. The Jewish chronology believes that the first language is Hebrew. There was no war before the Tower of Babel's fall. The people were united. Nimrod and Cush had no contenders vying for their position as leaders. The people were united. At first, they were even united in religious belief, that being the worship of Noah's God. This unity didn't change for at least 3 generations of people being born into the new civilization. Noah himself was revered and later, against his wishes, he was deified by some.

27a. **Africa:** Cush sailed from India around to colonize Ethiopia. H.I.H.Tafari Makonnen has compiled the first list of kings in Ethiopia. He published his list in 1922 A.D. Kam (Ham) and Kout (Cush) were the first two rulers of Ethiopia. Ethiopia later became the 25th Dynasty of Egypt during the Civil Wars of Egypt. Cush had a son, Sabta, who began to rule over Ethiopia after Cush left.

27b. **China:** Kusou (Cush) was the first ruler of China, a black man. The first religion of China was monotheistic and worshiped the unknown God of Noah. Ancestry worship became a big part of their religion very early on after they were established. Shoo King derived the king list which was later translated by Legge, *"Chinese Classic"*. Yao was the first oriental ruler after the first few western rulers. Shun Shun was the son of the first black ruler and Shun Shun was also black. His father was Kusou (Chusou) (Cush). His mother was called the "Queen of the West Land". Shun Shun is believed to be the same person as Nimrod. Shun Shun was believed to have ruled over both China and Babylon. Hoang Ti ruled right after Shun Shun (also a westerner) and he started the Xia Dynasty. This dynasty was at one time considered a myth, but archaeology has come to light to prove its existence. Hoang Ti was the first to establish the imperial yellow robes, albeit he was a westerner by appearance. His imperial seat was in Cho-Tong (Pe-Chi-Ling or Peking). The makes Peking one of the oldest known cities along with the Babylon cities. He built a temple of peace dedicated to the God of Noah. This tells us that Cush and Nimrod both were still worshippers of the God of Noah when they colonized China. Hoang Ti's wife discovered how to use the silk worm to make silk. After the fall of the Tower, Hoang Ti created the first Chinese Alphabet. He recorded the first Chinese calendar, consisting of 12 months, each with 30 days, so that the year consisted of 360 days. He later declared independence from the Babylon Empire of his father and started the first 60 year cycle in his 66th year. The last ruler of this dynasty and his wife put into practice sexual deviations never before heard of. The Chang Dynasty followed this dynasty.

Xia Dynasty	Years	Revised A.T. / B.C.	Xia Dynasty	Xia Dynasty	Years	Revised A.T. / B.C.
Kam	78	1658 / 2306	Ham	Shao K'ang	22	2113 / 1851
Kout or Chusou	50	1686 / 2278	Cush	Ch'u	17	2135 / 1829
Shun	50	1736 / 2228	Nimrod	Huai	26	2152 / 1812
Hoang-Ti	100	1786 / 2178	Westerner in appearance	Mang	18	2178 / 1786
Xia Dynasty starts when Hoang Ti breaks with Babylon Empire				Hsieh	16	2196 / 1768
Yao or Yaou	72	1886 / 2078	Chinese alphabet	Pu Chiang	59	2212 / 1752
Shun II	29	1958 / 2006		Chiung	21	2271 / 1693
Yu	8	1987 / 1977	First Chinese national	Chin	21	2292 / 1672
Ch'I / Ti-Ki	9	1995 / 1969		K'ung Chia	31	2313 / 1651
Tai K'ang	29	2004 / 1960	Conjunction of 5 planets.	Kao	11	2344 / 1620
Chung K'ang	13	2033 / 1931		Fa	19	2355 / 1609
Hsiang / Ti-Fyang	27	2046 / 1918		Chieh Kuei	52	2374 / 1590
Hong-Yi		2073 / 1891	Usurper to throne	1st cruel ruler of China.		
Han Cho	40	2073 / 1891	Usurper to throne	**To Shang Dynasty**		

27c. **Greece:** While Nimrod and Cush were rulers of the new world after the flood, their influence over Greece was less concentrated. Japheth, son of Noah, and his sons were the rulers over the European colonization. Not much is mentioned about Japheth and his sons in the Bible, so much of our information is extra-Biblical. Eusebius tells us that Sicyon is the oldest known civilization in Greece. The first ruler was around the same time as Nimrod. The area was named after the first ruler, Aegialeus. Syncellus places Aegialeus in the 76th year of Nahor I, but this seems a bit late. Africanus places Europs at the same time as Terah. James Ussher places Aegialeus 1313 years before the first Olympiad (776 B.C.). The name Aegialeus means *man of the coastland*. Ionians were closely behind Sicyon but more than likely they were developed at the same time. The mythological Atlantis was colonized by Evenor from the Aegean civilization according to Plato. The first date of invasion into Greece (not necessarily by war) was around 2200 B.C. which corresponds to the first populations after the flood. Atlantis was named after Atlas, the son of Evenor.

Sicyon is the first city known in Europe, as declared by Eusebius. Iolcus (built by another son of Japheth) was built about the same time, so that Sicyon and Iolcus existed about the same time as the first cities of

Greece. The archaeological support of the first cities is contradictory to historians who wish to disclaim the Bible as a valid history, and reduce it to mythology. The following from Eusebius:

"The Sicyonians and their kings are said to be the most ancient of the Greeks. The first king to rule Sicyon was Aegialeus, at the same time as Ninus and Belus, who are the first recorded kings of the Assyrians and of Asia. The Peloponnese was originally called Aegialeia, after this Aegialeus."

Berossus does not believe that Greece worshipped the pantheon of gods famous in Greek history. They were initially monotheistic taking after Noah's example. The Phoenicians and the Egyptians both vie for the position of introducing polytheism into Greece. This is believed to had taken place around the time of Cecrops of Athens, but this revised work believes that is far too late and polytheism existed before that. Temples for Jupiter are found to be dated much earlier than Athens. Egypt indicates that the first Athenians were Egyptians and this work agrees with that theory.

Early Kings of Sicyon: From John Jackson's interpretation of Syncellus (dating based on LXX).

Greek Name	Jackson (LXX / Yrs)	Hoeh	Eusebius / Castor	Africanus	James Ussher	Rev B.C.
Deucalion / Noah						2306
Iapheth (Japheth ben Noah)						
Iavan (Javan ben Japheth)						
Elisa / Aeolius						
Aegialeus (Considered first real king)	2171 / 52	2063	1656 / 13	1978	2089	2039
Europs	2119 / 45	2011	1643 / 11	1926	2037	2018

Telchin / Telchis	2074 / 20	1966	1632 / 5	1881	1992	1974
Apis (Argos Kings)	2054 / 25	1946	1627 / 6	1861	1972	1955
Thelxion	2029 / 52	1921	1621 / 26	1836	1947	1931
Aegydrus	1977 / 34	1869	1595 / 17	1784	1895	1880

27d. **North Africa (Mitzer):** While Cush was colonizing the east coast of Africa, to the north, Mitzraim, son of Ham, colonized the lower Nile (which is toward the Mediterranean Sea). There is one king in the SKL that gives the name City of Kham (Ham), Khamazi Land. Mitzraim might be related to Aegyptos, where Egypt got its name. One of the Ethiopian kings was also known as Aegyptos.

Genesis / Bereshit 10 indicates that the Pelishtim (Philistines) came from Mitzraim. Immanuel Velikovsky believes that the later Philistines came from Khar or the Carians who lived in Crete when Minos (Menes of Aggade) invaded Crete. The first known archaeological reference is found at the Temple of Ekron around the time of King David of Israel. Professor James Heinsch found the inscription in 1996 A.D.

Makonnen Kings	Years	Revised A.T. / B.C.	Makonnen Kings	Years	Revised A.T. / B.C.
1. Kham	78	1658 / 2306	13. Hohey	35	2011 / 1953
2. Kout (Cush)	50	1677 / 2287 *	14. Adglag	20	2045 / 1919
3. Habassi	40	1726 / 2238	15. Lakniduga	25	2064 / 1900
4. Sebtah (Son of 2.)	30	1765 / 2199	16. Manturay	35	2088 / 1876
5. Elektron	30	1794 / 2170	17. Rakhu	30	2122 / 1842
6. Neber	30	1823 / 2141	18. Sabe I	30	2151 / 1813
7. Amen	21	1852 / 2112	19. Azagan	30	2180 / 1784
8. Nehasset Nais (Q)	30	1872 / 2092	20. Sousel Atozanis	20	2209 / 1755
9. Horkam	29	1901 / 2063	21. Amen II	15	2228 / 1736
10. Saba II	30	1929 / 2035	22. Ramenpahte	20	2242 / 1722
11. Sofard	30	1958 / 2006	23. Wanuna	3 days	2261 / 1703
12. Askndou	25	1987 / 1977	24. Piori I	15	2261 / 1703

27e. **Canaan:** Canaan ben Ham was the cursed son and settled in the land known for his name. His people were called Amorites by the Babylonians and the Assyrians. There are references in the Assyrian records of invasions from the Amorites. The sons of Abraham were also called Amorites by the Assyrians.

27f. **India:** Cush and Nimrod settled the upper regions of India. India's true history didn't start until around 600 B.C. but they have king lists pre-dating this. The lists were used by L.Austine Waddell to match to the SKL and the IKL and the Aryan King List of India was able to fill in some holes in the SKL. The first rulers of India were white men, not the typical Indian features. The *Puranas (Aryan King List)* are ancient records and while India was subject to Babylon, they recorded the kings over Babylon as their own. Uruash was one of the first *true* rulers of India, separate from Babylon. He started the Paunch Dynasty of India. The early calendar of India was as the others, 360 days, but they divided their months into 15 days so that they had 24 months of 15 days instead of the typical 12 months.

28. Bereshit / Genesis 11: The chapter starts off by saying that the people migrated from the *east*. They came upon the Valley of Shinar. Shinar is in Babylon and if they came from the east, this means that Noah and his family settled off the Ark and moved further west. This is a ways off from the *current* mountain known as Ararat.

Chapter 10 indicates the amount of time that has passed from the time the ark landed until the building of the tower. By the time they started building the tower, Eber had been born and was probably old enough to have a son Peleg. It was said that the world was divided during the days of Peleg. Peleg was born a hundred years after the flood. The reason for the Tower is often *believed* to have been so that the people had a place to run to should HaShem ever flood the earth again. They built the tower in the plains instead of choosing some place higher, so this reason does not make sense. The Koran version does not include the tower, but does include the separation of languages.

Reverend Hislop and Berossus both believe that by the time of the building of the tower, Nimrod had started a secret society, the first religion that didn't worship HaShem. Nimrod's wife, Semiramis, was also known as Inanna has been related to Isis in Egyptian mythology. Nimrod took (kidnapped) her from Aratta as told in the *Epic of Enmekar and the Lord of Aratta. The Epic of Lugal-banda and Mount Hurrum* is an account of

Lugal-banda's involvement in the Aratta affair. Dr. David P. Livingston believes that Nimrod and Gilgamesh are the same person, both out to destroy the God of Noah, Huwawa. Both were crude base men, stealer of women. Both died a violent death. The revised chronology believes that Gilgamesh was the grandson of Nimrod.

The tower was a temple dedicated to the worship of Jupiter. The title of Nimrod and succeeding high priests was *Supreme Pontiff* which got carried down to where it was adopted by the Bishop of Rome before he became known as the Pope. This is believed to have been restored from the pre-flood cult of Tubal-Cain. The Chaldeans are believed to have been the first polytheistic believers. Nimrod's body has been found in the digs of Ur. David Rohl believes that the tower was built on the original site of Eridu, one of the first cities of the pre-flood era. There was a temple built there by Enoch ben Cain. Jeremiah 1:2 says that "*Bel is the confounder and Merodach is broken into pieces.*" Bel is an alternate name for Cush. Merodach is the Sumerian name for Jupiter and this temple was broken into pieces as Jeremiah indicates. The *Epic of Marduk* talks about the building of the "*house of the uplifted head*". This epic gives the same timeline, being built after the Deluge and the battle of Marduk / Tiamat (Jupiter / Saturn battle that caused the flood). Polyhistor and Berossus quote the Sybillean Oracles. "*All men spoke the same language when they started to build the tower to climb up to heaven. A huge wind overturned the tower and then they began to speak their own languages.*" They also report that Chiush (Cush) ruled for 4 ners after the Flood. Abydenus reports that after the Flood, the people became puffed up with pride thinking they were better than HaShem.

The people wanted to stay united. The tower was to be a sign for people. Megasthenes reports that it was Ham and Cush who started the building of the tower when Nimrod was young along with the fortifications around the temple. The walls were mainly to keep the wild beasts out which had started to become a problem. Eusebius reports that it was Semiramis who built the walls. The height of the tower is reported that it was so high, it took a year to get to the top.

Eber, son of Shelah, was likely the King of Ebrium, was born around the time of the building of the tower. *The Tablets of Ebla* list 5 kingdoms destroyed in the same order as Sodom, Gomorrah, Admah, Zeboiim, and Bela (Zoar). This list was found in 1973 A.D.

28a. ***Epic of Gilgamesh***: One of the oldest known archaeological documents ever found. It was written after the Tower of Babel was started, but not before it fell. In many of the details, the epic follows the story of the Torah/Bible. It names Babylon as the *city of gods*. He calls the tower *Esagila and Parakhu*. Marduk (Sumerian name of Jupiter) was the ruling god. Lilith is mentioned in the epic. Semiramis offered to be his lover, but he had seen what she did to her lovers and he would have nothing to do with her. Gilgamesh also went to meet Noah. Gilgamesh has been tied to the legendary Hercules of Phoenician repute. Polyhistor and Berossus quote the Sybillean Oracles. *"All men spoke the same language when they started to build the tower to climb up to heaven. A huge wind overturned the tower and then they began to speak their own languages."*

28b. **Peleg:** Peleg was born before the tower fell. *The Book of Jasher* says that it was Peleg who invented wedges and built the walls around the tower city. The fall of the tower took place during his days but before his brother Joktan was born. It is believed that the Phoenicians were named after Pelasgi or Peleg. *The Book of Jubilees* says that Reu was born after the fall of the tower, supporting the suspected dates of the fall of the tower. Reu married the daughter or Ur, the builder of the city of Ur.

CHAPTER 6

AGE OF NATIONS

29. Bereshit / Genesis 11:5-9: The Fall of the Tower of Babel: This is the next descent of HaShem and the descent was for the sins of mankind again. This time, the sin wasn't violence but arrogance. They built the tower against HaShem. His concern was that they were united as one, which seems good, but they were united *against* HaShem. He confused their languages, which is supported by archaeology. The first alphabets of the Greeks, Phoenicians, and Egyptians didn't appear until after the fall of the tower. The Torah says that this is why the city was named Babel, because they began to babel at one another without understanding. Historians would have you believe that the different languages developed slowly. There's not an ounce of evidence to support that and they ignore the supernatural influence of HaShem.

29a. **Alphabets and languages:** John Jackson points out from numerous sources that writing was not yet available. The Phoenicians and Egyptians attempt to claim that they had documents (in tablets) from before the flood which is possible. The Assyrians were the last of the main civilizations to get an alphabet. The Hebrew claim is that the Hebrew language was the 1st original language, but this also has not been verified. There are no documents of the Jews (until Moses) that can be found.

All of the original languages developed without vowels. Vowels weren't added until much later. That languages are copies of each other is questionable, but possible. Some languages are written right to left and some the opposite which belies copycat alphabets. Chinese is written top to bottom. Numbers were considered to be represented by letters of the alphabet in many cases, such as Hebrew and Greek. Herodotus says that Egyptians had 2 sorts of letters; sacred and vulgar. The sacred letters were only known to the priests and contained their secret doctrines, called *sacerdotal*. The vulgar letters were called *epistolic*.

29b. Fall of the Tower of Babel: The year is 1762 A.T. The date chosen is the year before Joktan was born, during the days of Peleg. James Ussher and the *"Book of Sothis"* both agree with this date. The fall took place 69 years after it was started. In Hebrew chronology, this event took place at the end of Peleg's days, during the time of Abraham (1996 A.M.). This doesn't fit with chronology time. Abraham went to see the Pharaoh after the division of languages.

The height of the tower is reputed to be almost 5 miles high. The Empire State Building is only 1 mile high. The Mexican account indicates that the tower was blown down by a fierce wind. The *Talmud* says that a third was burned, a third blown down, and the bottom third left standing. Apparently the storm that tore it down was worldwide as the *Popol Vul* (Mayan document) indicates that after the darkness of the storm lifted no one could understand one another. Josephus and *Sibylline Oracles* confirm the strong winds that tore the tower down. Abraham Rockenbach, *"De Cometus Tractatus Novus Methodicus"*, connects the events with a comet. He believes these events took place 288 years after the flood. The comet passed through 3 constellations. The comet was called Typhon (later renamed as Venus). This comet was close enough to earth to cause huge storms all over the planet, and including the Plain of Shinar. It is possible that Cush died during the storm events as well. He died in violent events possibly at sea.

29c. Cosmology and Mythology: Venus and Mars were both comets at this time, circling the sun and then around out toward Jupiter, which was closer to earth than it is now. The mythology indicates that Neptune and Pluto (Poseidon and Hades) revolted against Jupiter. It is suggested here that the cosmological events caused the huge storms on earth. Rockenbach attaches this event to the events of the tower. He describes one of the influential planets as being Saturn like, which describes Neptune which also has rings. All of this evidence suggests that the solar system has not always been the same as it is in our current time. Ancient star maps from this time do not show either Venus or Mars. Jupiter and Moon worship were the most predominant gods in the land. Sun worship was there, but not predominant as might suggest by its size. Ancient tablets from China, Babylon, China, and the Mayans suggest that Venus did not exist in ancient times before the Tower of Babel. In Assyria, it is believed that Mars became their first god instead of following after the god of the Temple of Babel, Jupiter. Mars was named after Asher ben Shem, Azar or Ashar) in Sumerian.

The tower was destroyed by high winds, lightening, and fire. Abraham Rockenbach, *"De Cometis Tractatus Novus Methodicus"*, connects the confusion of tongues and languages to a comet that had Saturn like characteristics. His date is given as 1944 A.M. or 288 years after the flood (1656 A.M.). The comet passed through 3 constellations in the skies in 65 days. He called the comet Typhon.

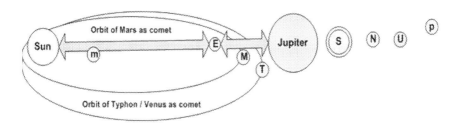

29d. Empires: While cities were developed during the years after the flood, the empires started to develop after the confusion of tongues. Conflicts arose and territory became precious. The Babylonian Empire really starts to form after the fall of the Tower, but the different city-kingdoms still maintain separate kings. The days of the united empire under Cush and Nimrod are over as the separation of nations by language started to create the development of new empires. This is about the time that China broke free of Babylon. Greece is developing and separates from Babylon. The local areas of Phoenicia, India and Egypt are still basically under the Babylon umbrella.

29e. Babylon: Kish I, Uruk (Erech) I and Ur I all developed under the Babylon umbrella. While one ruler still maintained rule over the three, they also developed local kings or governors. Semiramis declares war on her sons in Assyria and kills several of her sons, but one of her sons eventually kills her. She is the first known ruler (over Nineveh) to declare war. In particular, she declared war on the Babylonian territory of India but she lost the war according to Cephalion.

Cephalion indicates that there is a 1000 years between her and King Mitraeus. Status Quo history indicates that the small little known kingdom of Mari was much later, but evidence has revealed that it was developing alongside of Ur and the two of them had a few small skirmishes.

Revised King list of Kish: Names from different lists are matched phonetically or by *meaning*.

Austine Waddell		Conventional SKL	Lagash	Biblical and others	Years	Revised A.T. / B.C.
Kish	Uruk					
Not Listed				Ham, Kham	20 ?	1658 / 2306
Ga'ur, Gishur	Agush, Meskiagkasher	Gisur	Gurshur	Cush	18 ?	1677 / 2287
Mukhla, Azag, Gan	Mukh, Gan, Kan, Nimrud	Enmekar, Gan	Gunidu	Nimrod	52	1694 / 2270
Umanshe	Lugla-banda, Unnusha	Lugal-banda	Ur-Nanshe	Lugalbanda	25	1745 / 2219
Uda, Yadu, Yayati					6	1769 / 2195 *
Dumuzi, Jaya	Dumuzi, Dum-Gin	En-dara	Akurgal	Tammuz	10	1769 / 2195 *
Wishtara, Uziwitar					6	1778 / 2186
Ma, Babum		Babum	Eannatum		11	
Piash-enzu		Pa-annum	Enannatum I		11	
Sumaddi, Nashu	Sumanta	Kalibum	Entemena		3	
Burudu Prithu		Kalumum	Enannatum II			
Dudu Mumu, Gautama		Zuqa qip	Lugallanda			
Azag, Agga of Kish		Atab, Azag	Enetazi	Gilgamesh		1784 / 2180
Arwasag	Uruash, Ur-Nunga	Uruash Kha	Uruk gina	Ur-Nungal		1822 / 2142

Standard List of Kish and Uruk

Isin King Lists		Sumerian Inscriptions	Aryan King List
Kish	Uruk		
Arwasag	Uruash	Uruash	Haryashva
Gal, Lora, Ma-rud	Mukh	Madgal	Mudgala, Maru
Bagu	Baussa	Bi-ashnadi, Bisar	B'adry, B'ujyu
Enishib, Enme	Ennun-nad	Enash-nadi	Yuvan-ashva
Mede	Mede	Medi or Meti	Mettiyo
Ga'ag, Mug	Kiaga	Ki-aga	Mucu-kunda
Dixsaax		Tarsi, Shudig	Sudasa
Tizama			Tzomaka
		Anta	Jantu

29f. Egypt: While not an established self-ruling empire, early Egypt is believed to have had its start around this time. James Ussher believes the first kingdom of Egypt started around 2188 A.M. based on a reference from Constantinus Manasses. Manasses claims that Egypt started 1663 years before Cambyses of Persia. David Down and John Ashton place Egypt around 2109 B.C. The history of Egypt has centered on the records of Manetho although it is well known to have flaws. The dynasty breaks of Egypt are the creation of modern historians.

Egypt's beginning dates by different historians

Historian	Date	Historian	Date
Waddell	2704 B.C.	Manetho	2234 B.C.
Manasses	2188 B.C.	Rohl	2770 B.C.
Josephus	2300 B.C.	Down / Ashton	2100 B.C.
Syncellus	2776 B.C.	Sargon	22nd year
Erastostbenes	2220 B.C.	Revised	2023 A.T
Jackson	2234 B.C.	Revised	1941 B.C.

Manetho No.	Nebty Name	David Rohl Pre-Dynasty	Austine Waddell	
1	Har Sekah	Har Sekah		
2	Har Khaya	Har Khaya		
3	Har Teyew	Har Teyew		
4	Har Tjesh	Har Tjesh		
5	Har Neheb	Har Neheb		
6	Har Waznez	Har Waznez		
7	Har Mekh	Har Mekh		
		Rohl Dynasty 0	**Austine Waddell**	
N/A	Har Sarek Scorpion	2830 B.C.		
8	Har Sekhen	2815 B.C.	Tukh or Dukh	Grandfather
9	Har Irihar	2810 B.C.	Ro Buru-gin	Father
10	Har Ka	2800 B.C.	Har Ka'ap Sargon	Sargon
N/A	Har Narmer	2785 B.C.		

The Turin Canon lists the kings of Egypt without any such dynasties, one long list of kings. There are many illegible names on the Turin list and many missing kings. As with the Assyrian records, the biggest problem with Egyptian history is translating the ancient Egyptian language. Without accurate keys, many historians translated the same name differently and thus created many people from one actual person. Courville, Dr. John Bimson, and Damien Mackay are just 3 historians attempting to revise the Egyptian history mistakes. Waddell recognized that lists of pre-dynasty 1 kings were written in the walls of the temples at Abydos in Sumerian. Their names started with the prefix *Hor* which is an alternate name for Ham. David Rohl places the beginning of the pre-dynasty period in 2850 B.C. around the time of Lugalbanda's 12th year.

Sargon of Agade is the father of Menes/Manas-Tishu who was the first pharaoh of traditional dynasty 1. Like Nimrod, the kings listed below were considered priest-kings. It is believed here that Menes rebelled against his father, Sargon, and started Egypt off as a separate nation. Sargon's name Har Kha is written on the walls of Abydos in Egypt and his body and that of his wife, Lady Ash, was buried in Abydos in Egypt. Their inscriptions were written in Sumerian, not Egyptian. They are the first known Pharaohs (Pra) of Egypt. Manas-Tishu was the royal heir of Sargon's kingdom, but he rebelled against his father and went to live in Abydos. The writings on the temples and walls by Menes (Manas) are in the same direction as Sumerian, not typical Egyptian. Menes' son rescued Sargon's stolen horses and he became heir to Sargon's kingdom in place of his son.

Revised list of pre-dynasty kings of Egypt: Egypt is a territory of Agade/ Babylon at this time and not a self-ruling kingdom.

Revised Egypt Pre-Dynasty List	Revised A.T. / B.C.	Notes
Ham, Kham, or Hor (also Her or Har)	1664 / 2300	Son of Noah
Mitzraim	1714 / 2250	Son of Ham
Taaut or Patruism		
Lost list of rulers		
Har Sekah / Saki		

Har Khaya / Kan or Gan		This bears a resemblance to Nimrod's other names
Har Teyew / Aja		
Har Tjesh / Uruash		He ruled over Kish, indicating that Egypt is a part of the Babylon Empire
Har Neheb		
Har Waznex / Weneg		
Har Mekh / Mukh		Another name from the Babylon Kish list
Har Sekhen / Khetem, Tuhk, Tug		Grandfather of Sargon
Har Irihar / Urudu-Gin, Puru-Gin, Ro	1973 / 1991	Father of Sargon, defeated by Lugalzagissi
Lugal-zagissi	1987 / 1977	Usurper over Babylon in Ur
Har Kha / Sargon I	2012 / 1952	Ruled from Agade or Accad. Egypt is a part of the Babylon Empire.

29g. Assyria: It would appear that the different sources give us two immediate lines for the Assyrians, but both lines lived in the same area of north Mesopotamia. One was the line of Asher ben Shem, which is interpreted here to be the Assyrians who lived in tents for the 1st dynasty. The 2nd line was from the city of Nineveh which was built by Nimrod. James Ussher copies Theophilus in reporting that Nineveh was built 1903 years before Alexander the Great (331 B.C.). The 1st real city of Nineveh is completed in 2234 B.C., some number of years before Nimrod died. The Biblical account indicates that he built Nineveh after establishing the kingdoms of Babylon and Agade, which is in agreement with Ussher's dating for Nineveh. This results in 2 different king lists for Assyria, 2 different lines.

The deification of Semi-ra-mis was her own doing, according to Rev. Hislop. He believes that she had herself and Nimrod deified after Nimrod died a violent death. She had an illegitimate son by her own son, Lugalbanda. She declared that the illegitimate son was the reincarnation of Tammuz or Nimrod reincarnated, giving rise to the stories of yearly resurrection of Tammuz (equated to Osiris tales in Egypt and later referenced by Ezekiel the prophet). This son was Dumuzi in the king list. She ruled alongside of Lugalbanda until he too died a violent death (possibly by her hand).

The story of Semiramis is by no means the story of a docile and passively ruling queen. She took the kingdom of Nineveh for her own, leaving most of the empire to Lugalbanda. They co-ruled the kingdom, but from the lists and history, it would seem that Lugalbanda and Dumuzi were the true rulers. She declared war on India, which at that time was under the main empire rule of Lugalbanda / Dumuzi. This supports the idea that she was a strong ruler of Assyria. The interpretation taken here is that her only kingdom was that of Assyria, as supported by Eusebius and his ancient sources. The records of Diodorus tell us that Ninus was before Semiramis, not after, so Ninyas cannot be the same person as Ninus (who is Nimrod). The reports are that she killed her sons in order to rule (Berossus and Eusebius), but this must have been after they had already ruled for a number of years. They indicate that Lugalbanda and Dumuzi (sons of Nimrod and Semiramis) ruled over the empire. It is believed here that the rumors of her killing her sons are due to her actions to *deify herself in Nineveh.* She wanted Nimrod and her son (illegitimate by Lugalbanda), Ninyas to become like gods worshipped by the people. According to the following list, Gilgamesh was a son of Semiramis. Incest not being an issue, she wanted to be his lover too, but he had seen what happened to her lovers and refused her attentions.

Assyrian King List by Ctesias: Nineveh

Eusebius (Eusebius notes)	Ctes. BC	Rev B		Eusebius	Ctes. BC	Rev B
Belus / Cush		2287		Lamprides	1391	1497
Ninus / Nimrod	2127	2172		Sosmares	1359	1460
Building of Nineveh		2234		Lampares	1339	1440
Semiramis I (started age 20)	2075	2120		Pannias (Argonauts)	1309	1410
Zames or Ninyas (Gilgames)	2006	2078		Sosanus	1264	1368
Arius (Awrawasag)	1968	2040		Mithraeus	1245	1349
Aralius or Amyrus (Maru)	1938	2010		Arabelus	1220	Only found in
Xerxes or Balaeus (Balih)	1898	1970		Chalaus	1178	Syncellus
Armamithres (Mitrayu)	1868	1940		Anebus	1133	account of
Belochus (Messapus)	1830	1902		Babius	1095	Ctesius
Balacaus	1795	1867		Teutamus (Troy)	1178	1312
Aladas / Sethos / Zaztagus	1743	1855		Teutaeus	1134	1280
Mamythus	1708	1820		Theneus	1104	1240
Machchaelaeus	1678	1790		Dercylus (Not in most vrsns)		1210
Spherus	1648	1760		Eupalmes (Time of David)	1064	1170
Mamylus	1628	1738		Laosthenes	1026	1132
Sparaethus / Spareus	1598	1708		Peritiades	981	1087
Ascatades (Time of Moses)	1556	1666		Ophrataeus	951	1057
Amyntas	1518	1626		Ophatanes	930	1036
Belochus (Time of Perseus)	1473	1576		Acrazanes	878	986
Balatores	1425	1531		Sardanapallus / Sardan Pul	836	944
				First Olympiad after Sardan	776	884

Asher Line of Kings:

Kings from Asher ben Shem who lived in Tents (1 – 27)			Last 3 Kings
1. Tudiya or Dudiya	12. Nuabu	23. Ilu-mer	34. Erishum
2. Adamu	13. Abazu	24. Hajanu	35. Ikunum
3. Yangi or Janqi	14. Belu	25. Samanu	36. Sargon I of Agade
4. Kitlamu or Sahlamu	15. Azarah	26. Hale	
5. Harharu	16. Uspija	10 King Ancestors	
6. Mandaru	17. Apiasal	28. Zariqum	
7. Imsu	18. Aminu	29. Kikkija	
8. Harsu	19. Ila-kabkabi	30. Akija	**Kings on bricks (28 – 33)**
9. Didanu (Dedan of Bible)	20. Jazkur-ilu	31. Puzur Ashur I	
10. Hanu	21. Jakmeni	32. Shalim-Ahu	
11. Zuabu	22. Jakmesi	33. Ilu-Shuma	

29h. Yemen / Arab Princes: James Ussher and Louis Ginzberg believes that Noah took his family to the plain of Shinar after they landed. He divided the land up between his 3 sons and it was up to them to divide the land further. The Bible indicates that they came from the east and then they decided to build the tower. The period between the two sentences consists of many years of time.

Peleg was the older brother of Joktan. It was from Joktan that the first Arabians began. Ishmael, ben Abraham, was the progenitor of the Arabs at a later date. The first known Aramaeans came from Joktan. Herman Hoeh traces the following list of Yemen princes and Arabian princes (two lines).

Yemen Princes	Arabian Princes
Joktan, bro of Peleg	
Yarab	Jorham, bro of Yarab
Yashab	Abd Yalil
Abd Shems	Jorsham
Hamyar	Abdo'l Masih
Wayel	Modad
Alsacsac	Amru I
Yaafar	Al Hareth
Dhu Rujash	Amru II
Al Numan	Basher
Ashman	Modad
Shaddad, during Hyksos	Kedar ben Ishmael

29i. China: The first histories believes that Shun ruled over China for 50 years. This agrees with the approximate time that Nimrod ruled over Babylon. The revised dates for China's Xia Dynasty are based on dates from the following dynasty, the Shang Dynasty which is matched to events against the famine of Joseph.

Xia Dynasty	Years	Revised A.T. / B.C.	Xia Dynasty
Kam	78	1658 / 2306	Ham
Kout or Chusou	50	1686 / 2278	Cush
Shun	50	1736 / 2228	Nimrod
Hoang-Ti	100	1786 / 2178	Westerner in appearance
Xia Dynasty starts when Hoang Ti breaks with Babylon Empire			
Yao or Yaou	72	1886 / 2078	Chinese alphabet
Shun II	29	1958 / 2006	
Yu	8	1987 / 1977	First Chinese national
Ch'I / Ti-Ki	9	1995 / 1969	
Tai K'ang	29	2004 / 1960	Conjunction of 5 planets.
Chung K'ang	13	2033 / 1931	
Hsiang / Ti-Fyang	27	2046 / 1918	
Hong-Yi		2073 / 1891	Usurper to throne
Han Cho	40	2073 / 1891	Usurper to throne

Xia Dynasty	Years	Revised A.T. / B.C.
Shao K'ang	22	2113 / 1851
Ch'u	17	2135 / 1829
Huai	26	2152 / 1812
Mang	18	2178 / 1786
Hsieh	16	2196 / 1768
Pu Chiang	59	2212 / 1752
Chiung	21	2271 / 1693
Chin	21	2292 / 1672
K'ung Chia	31	2313 / 1651
Kao	11	2344 / 1620
Fa	19	2355 / 1609
Chieh Kuei	52	2374 / 1590
1st cruel ruler of China.		
To Shang Dynasty		

29j. Greece: Among the sons of Japheth, a group later called the Khar or Carians settled the island of Crete. They were mainly pirates (after the flood). The Khar ruled the island of Crete before the Minoans. Toward the mainland, the Ionians and the Sicyonians were the two earliest kingdoms in Greece. Noah was recognized as an early ruler over the Greeks, but it isn't known if he ever lived there.

The most ancient of Greeks all used a 360 day calendar according to Orpheus, one of the most ancient of poets and astrologers. Cleobulus used this fact in a popular riddle in his day. An ancient constitution of Athens (dated much later than the early Greeks) found by Harpocration Julius Pollux gives the same configuration for a year in Athens.

Greek Name	Biblical match	A.T.
Deucalion	Noah	1660 A.T. (?)
Iapheth	Japheth	1700 A.T. (?)
Iavan	Javan	
Elisa or Aeolius	Elisha	

Sicyon Early Kings: J.J. = John Jackson; H.H. = Herman Hoeh; E/C = Eusephius / Castor; J.A. = Julius Africanus; J.U. = James Ussher. Jackson is based on the LXX version. The dates for Aegialus are fixed for Ussher and Africanus against the dates of Nahor I. All dates are B.C. except Revised dates. Agamemnon invaded from Argos and defeated Hippolytus without a fight.

Greek Kings	J.J.	H.H.	E/C	J.A.	J.U.	Revised A.T. / B.C.
Aegialeus	2171	2063	1656	1978	2089	1925 / 2039
Europs	2119	2011	1643	1926	2037	1946 / 2018
Telchin / Telchis	2074	1966	1632	1881	1992	1990 / 1974
Apis	2054	1946	1627	1861	1972	2009 / 1955
Thelxion	2029	1921	1621	1836	1947	2033 / 1931
Aegydrus	1977	1869	1595	1784	1895	2084 / 1880
Thurimachus	1943	1835	1578	1750	1861	2117 / 1847
Leucippus	1898	1790	1555	1705	1816	2161 / 1803
Messapus	1845	1737	1529	1652	1763	2213 / 1751
Eratus / Peratus	1798	1690	1505	1605	1716	2259 / 1705
Plemnaeus	1752	1644	1482	1559	1670	2304 / 1660

Orthopolis	1704	1596	1458	1511	1622	2351 / 1613
Marathonius	1641	1533	1427	1448	1559	2413 / 1551
Marathus	1611	1503	1412	1418	1529	2442 / 1522
Echyreus	1591	1483	1402	1398	1509	2451 / 1513
Corax	1536	1428	1374	1343	1454	2505 / 1459
Laomedon (1st)		1398				No first time
Epopeus / Apophis	1506	1358	1359	1313	1424	2513 / 1451
Laomedon (2nd)	1471	1326	1342	1278	1389	2575 / 1389
Sicyon	1431	1322	1322	1238	1349	2594 / 1370
Polybus	1386	1277	1277	1193	1304	2638 / 1326
Inachus	1346	1238	1233	1153	1264	2677 / 1287
Phaestus	1304	1196	1191	1111	1222	2718 / 1246
Adrastus	1296	1188	1183	1103	1214	2275 / 1239
Polypheides	1292	1183	1179	1099	1210	2728 / 1236
Pelagus	1261	1152	1148	1068	1179	2758 / 1206
Zeuxippus	1241	1132	1132	1048	1159	2774 / 1190
Phaestus	1209	1101	1101	1016	1128	2779 / 1185
Rhopalus						
Hippolytus						

Herman Hoeh matches Epopeus to Apophis (18 in the list) of the Hyksos invaders and it would appear that the Hyksos invaders of Egypt ruled over most of Europe for several hundred years. James Ussher's dates match well to this conclusion. Elisa or Elisha is one of the sons of Javan and one of the first settlers of the Greek area. There is about a 200 year gap between him and the first known / registered Sicyon king. Due to the lack of languages being established, there is no record of the kings during this time.

29k. Kish II or Babylon Continued: Conventional historians believe that Kish II were subject to Lagash. According to this revised list, Lagash rulers and Kish I rulers were the same people. This list fell right on the heels of Ur I and probably co-existed with Ur I if not also being the same rulers. The last 2 rulers conventionally fall as early rulers of Uruk II. Baragin or Puru-gin was the father of Sargon. Lugal-zagissi defeated him and ruled as usurper to the throne for 25 years. Sargon was just a new born at the time and his mother fled with him. When he grew to be 25 years of age, Sargon formed an army and defeated Lugal-zagissi and took back his father's throne. Lugal-zagissi ruled over the Babylon Empire from Ur rather than Agade or Kish. Lugal conquered the Sicyonians and made them shave their heads. There are several references to the Sicyonians having had to shave their heads. Lugalzagissi's name was left out of the Aryan King List because he was a usurper and not considered a true king.

Kish II Conventional and Revised: Roux and Rohl dates are B.C. Tug or Tukh also ruled as a pre-dynasty king of Egypt at Abydos. His name has been found there written in Sumerian. Tukh is the grandfather of Sargon in this revised version. This listing shows the matched names in Uruk during this time.

Sumerian King List	George Roux for SKL	David Rohl for SKL	Uruk in Isin King List	Estimated Revised A.T. / B.C.
Susuda	2500	2397	Susuda at Kish	1884 / 2080 ?
Dadase Dadasig		2377	Dudu, Gun-gun	
Magalgalla		2357	Mama-gal	
Kalbum		2321	Kalbu, so of Mama-gal	
Tug, Tukh		2302	Tuke	
Men-nuna, Bara-gin		2266	Buru-gin, Puru-gin	Puru-gin 1964 / 2010
Enbieshtar	2430	2248		Puppet of Lugalgu
Lugalgu		2228-2193		Lugal-zagissi 1979 / 1985

Sargon wrote an autobiography about how his mother fled the usurper Lugal and he was raised by Anakki, a fire priest (not coincidentally, Ur was called the city of fire. Later the Bible says that Abraham was called out of the fire). After Sargon defeated Lugal-zagissi, he ruled for 54 years according to his own hand. By his 11th year, he ruled from Egypt to India and everything in between. There is no mention of his ruling over China or Greece. Under his rule, the empire was prosperous but not without uprisings and revolts. During his time, the Guti, a barbaric tribe, grew more powerful in the Hittite area of Carchemish. The Guti eventually became the Goths of Europe. They eventually overcame Akkad, when it was being ruled by Sar-Kali-Sarri, a descendent of Sargon.

Sargon and his wife lived many years in Abydos, even though he and his son, Menes, were at war with one another. He died there and all of his inscriptions in Abydos are in Sumerian.

One of Sargon's records about his conquests:

"Afterwards, he the land of the Good Edin City attacked. They submitted to his arms. And King Gin settled that revolt and defeated them. He achieved their overthrow and their wide spreading host, he destroyed." The equivalent record in the *Omens of India* reads as follows: *"King Ginna* (another name for Sargon) *the land of the Good Edin City in its might he attacked. They submitted to his arms. And King Ginna smote them grievously and defeated them…"*

Conventional and Revised Agade Dynasty of Babylonian Empire:
C.D. = Conventional Date; G.R. = George Roux; D.R. = David Rohl; A.W. = Austine Waddell. All dates in B.C. except Revised.

Sumerian King List	C.D.	G.R.	D.R.	A.W.	Waddell from IKL / KC / AKL	Revised A.T. / B.C.	
Sargon	2334	2334	2117	2725	Gunni, Shar-gani	2003 / 1961	
Menes ben Sargon rebelled and ruled Egypt apart from his father						2022 / 1942	
Rimus / Rimush	2278	2278	2061	2670	Mush, Lugalgu	2055 / 1909	
Manishtusu / Menes	2269	2269	2052	2655	Masshu, Manis-tusu	2063 / 1901	
Naram-Sin ben Menes	2254	2254	2037	2640	Naram, Lord Enzu	2077 / 1887	
Sar-Kali-Sarri	2217	2217	2000	2584		2079 / 1885	
Irigigi / Igigi/ Elulu	2192		1975	2560		2080 / 1884	Great famine
Nanum		Anar-	1975	2560			
Imi		chy	1975	2560		Gutium Rule	
Elulu							

This leads to a revised list of rulers over the world from the Babylon center, and the following list gives this revised interpretation of an unbroken list of rulers. Other rulers ruled from small city-kingdoms but they were subject to the overall Babylon Empire. In the following chart, the "Matches to others" indicates that there was some archaeological connection between the ruler and the matched person. This doesn't mean that their dates of existence were exact. Abraham for instance is believed to have been just a boy when Sargon ruled having been born 5 years after Sargon began to rule.

Revised complete Babylon Empire rulers to Agade Empire

Revised Babylonian Empire	Revised A.T. / B.C.	Matches to others	Sumerian King List	Revised A.T. / B.C.	Matches to others
Cush	1677 / 2287	Arpachshad ben Shem	Dadase, Dudu, Gun-gun		
Nimrod	1694 / 2270		Mama-gal, Vijaya		
Lugal-banda	1745 / 2219		Tuke		Tai K'ang of China
Uda	1769 / 2195		Puru-gin, Ur-Nina, Bara	1964 / 2000	
Tammuz / Dumuzi	1769 / 2195	Eber ben Peleg	Lugal-zagissi, Zagissi	1979 / 1985	
Uziwitar	1778 / 2186		Sargon, Shar-gun, Kha-gin	2003 / 1961	Abraham ben Terah
Gilgamesh, Azag	1784 / 2180		Rimush ben Sargon	2055 / 1909	
Uruash, Arwasag	1822 / 2142		Manish-tusu ben Sargon	2063 / 1901	Menes / Minos same
Mukh, Madgal, Etana			Naram-Sin	2077 / 1887	Over Egypt too
Medi of Kish			Sar-kali-sarri	2079 / 1885	
Ki-Aga, Mug			Igigi	2080 / 1884	Probably only Egypt
Tarsi, Shu-dig, Su-dasa			Gutium Rule	2079 / 1885	

Many of the other kings in the SKL were kings alongside or co-rulers. This list is the estimated list of absolute rulers over the Empire.

29k. Royal Line of Abraham: The ancestors of Abraham have been listed with their years of birth (see Section 25). Modern Christians have tried to manipulate the line of Abraham's ancestors and tried to make them seem *holy*. This is not the case. Serug learned about astrology and taught it to his son, Nahor I. Terah, the father of Abraham, was a maker of idols which he sold during the time of Sargon. Terah lived in a small village outside of Ur (verified by Joshua 24:2) and it is believed that he supplied moon idols for the Temple of the Moon there, where Sargon's daughter was the high priestess.

Post-Flood Patriarchs: Masor. = Masoretic Text; LXX = Septuagint; Euseb. = Eusebius.; Samar. = Samaritan Text; JUB = Book of Jubilee; JU= James Ussher; Rohl = David Rohl; Rev = this revised work, based on Masoretic Text. Shem lived throughout the lives of all of the Patriarchs of this list. He died during the lifetime of Abraham.

Patriarch	Masor. A.M.	LXX A.M.	LXX Euseb.	Samar A.M.	JUB A.M.	J.U. B.C.	Rohl B.C.	Rev B.C.
Arpachshad ben Shem	1658	2264	2264	1309	1429	2346	3011	2306
Cainan ben Ham		2399						
Shelah ben Arpachshad	1693	2529	2399	1444	1432	2311	2746	2271

Eber ben Shelah	1723	2659	2529	1574	1499	2281	2616	2241
Peleg ben Eber	1757	2793	2663	1708	1567	2247	2482	2207
Reu ben Peleg	1787	2923	2793	1838	1628	2217	2352	2177
Serug ben Reu	1819	3055	2928	1970	1687	2185	2222	2145
Nahor ben Serug (I)	1849	3185	3058	2100	1800	2155	2090	2115
Terah ben Nahor I	1878	3264	3137	2179	1806	2126	1970	2086

The list of Terah's sons are given in order of importance rather than order of birth. Abraham is listed first and as such, is accepted by the Jewish Chronology as being born in 1948 A.M., the year of the firstborn of Terah. It is here that this revised history departs from the chronology dates of the Jewish established Seder.

Birth Yr. A.T.	Entry to Canaan	Exodus Year	Iyyar 16th of Exodus Year (start of manna)	Day of Week of Iyyar 16th
1948	2023	2453	882766	Tuesday
2008	2083	2513	904366	Sunday

Abraham's birth is necessary for an accurate dating of the first fall of manna during the time of Moses. Sunday is the day for Manna to start falling. They gathered for 6 days and on the 7th they went out again. This angered HaShem because it was the Sabbath. The *Chinese Bamboo Annals* says that when Abram was born, there was a giant start. Sedar Olam has Abram being born on Tishrei 15th. *Book of Jubilees* says that he was named after his mother's father. Abram was married 2 full years after Noah's death.

Sarah is the key to knowing that Abraham could not have been born in 1948 A.T. She is 10 years younger than Abraham and would have been born in 1958 A.T. According to the number of her years of living, she would have died a mere 2 years after Terah. This does not allow her time to have a son after Abraham's other son, Ishmael. She could not have died this soon after Terah. Further verses indicates that Abraham was 75 when his father died. Since Terah died at the age of 205, this indicates that Abraham was born when Terah was 130 years old.

The Midrash has all three sons born within 4 years of each other (1948 A.M.) In order for this to happen, Haran would have been 6 years old when Lot was born. Haran was the one born in 1948, and his two brothers were born over 60 years later. Haran died in Ur. Some sources indicate that he died in a fire that was caused by Abram. Haran's son, Lot, was a little younger than Abram, but about the same age.

Abram is the father of two major factions, the Jews and the Arabs which today has evolved into the Muslims. Both factions recognize Abraham as their father. Islam recognizes Ibrahim as a prophet of ancient Muslim. They have a holy day in honor of Ibrahim. They believe Abraham created the city of Hijazi which is Mecca. They recognize that Ibrahim asked HaShem to bless both his sons, Ismael (the progenitor of the Muslims) and Isaac (the progenitor of the Jews). At this time both factions were at peace. The Muslim story of Abraham and his two wives follows closely with the Jewish version of the Torah. They agree that Abraham's father was an idolater. They have a story about Abraham to be burned at the stake by Nimrod, but their history does not follow. Nimrod was long dead by the time Abraham was born. They do have another story that Abraham, frustrated by his father's false gods, was spoken to by HaShem who told him to become a Muslim. This is a little hard to swallow as the Muslim religion didn't start until around 600 A.D.

Preview of Jewish history

1993 Years / Times of the Jews			
430 years	430 years	430 years	Time of Gentiles
75	Patriarch Period	Judge Period	King Period	Exile Period

Entry to Canaan — Exodus — Israel requests a king — Destruction of Jerusalem — Crucifixion of Yeshua

2008 A.T.

4000 A.T.

Age of Promise	Age of Law	Age of Grace

30. Menes of Agade: Menes rebelled against Sargon. L. Austine Waddell tied Menes to Manishtusu son of Sargon. They both have the same seal and this seal has been found in India, Egypt, Agade, and Crete. Sargon exiled his son and Menes went to Egypt taking a large army with him to Abydos. It is believed that Menes built the city of Memphis as well. They were at war with one another, but surprisingly, it was also known that the two would get together for casual meetings, based on references for both. In the last of his days, Sargon and his wife, lived in Abydos with his son. The revolt started in the 20th year of Sargon. It was 2 years later that Egypt declared sovereignty from Agade/Babylon. This was in 2025 A.T. and Abraham was about 17 years of age at the beginning of Egyptian's true history under Menes. Menes had a black obelisk that was discovered by De Morgan in 1897 at Susa. On it, Menes records about his purchase of property in Agade. Menes ruled for Sargon's last 35 years in Egypt. The clothing, art, and burial styles of Dynasty 1 of Egypt are the same styles as those in Ur. Even more striking, Menes' statues have blue eyes, not the normal eyes for an Egyptian, but very normal for a Chaldean. Menes died at the work of a hippopotamus in the river Nile.

In conventional Egyptian history, Dynasty 1 and 3 are separated by Dynasty 2. Dynasty 2 doesn't fit here as the art and burial styles are different, whereas the styles of Dynasty 1 and 3 are exactly the same. It is the conclusion here that Dynasty 3 is part of Dynasty 1. Many of the kings of Dynasty 3 actually belong to Dynasty 4. This is a big leap from conventional Egyptian history. It is the famine that ties both Dynasty 1 and 3 together. Modern historians have a famine in both dynasties and both famines last 7 years, but there is only a record of 1 major famine at this time and it started in Babylon. Dr. Courville makes a record of the revolt in Dynasty 3, but the revolt was not against Egypt, but against Agade. While Menes broke from his father, Sargon, the complete break from Agade rule didn't take place until Dudu (Teti). The conventional Dynasty 4 followed this revised dynasty.

Combining dynasties 1 and 3 into one moves the first dynasty into the Middle Kingdom which means that building pyramids is no longer a mystery. The increased technology allows the making of pyramids more comprehensible. This work is not the first time this merge of dynasties has been considered. Dr. Donovan Courville, *The Exodus problems and its ramifications,* believes that they are either the same or they run parallel at the same time. This also removes an extraneous 600 years of Egyptian history that did not really take place, and has led to a matching period of *dark ages* in Greek history which could not be easily matched to Egyptian history. These dark ages in Greek history simply go away and do not exist.

Revised Egypt Dynasty 1	A.T. / B.C.	Revised Agade	A.T. / B.C.
Har Ka / Shar-gun	2014 / 1950	Sargon, Shar-gun, Kha-gin	2003 / 1961
Menes / Har Aha Mena	2022 / 1942	Rimush ben Sargon	2055 / 1909
Menes / Har Mena over world	2063 / 1901	Manish-tusu ben Sargon	2063 / 1901
Narmer Teti / Har Ateti	2077 / 1887	Naram-Sin	2077 / 1887
Khent / Har Kenty / Shar-Guni	2083 / 1881	Sar-kali-sarri	2079 / 1885
Uenephes / Bagid / Igigi / Zoser	2080 / 1884	Igigi	2080 / 1884
World wide famine 2082 – 2089 / 1882 – 1875			
Dudu Usaph / Ba Teti	2098 / 1866	Egypt broke off from Agade	

Waddell's version of Egypt Dynasty 1

Babylon Name	SKL Name	AKL Name	Petrie	Budge	Manetho
Manistusu	Manj, Ahaman	Asa Manj	Nor-mer	Aha	Menes
Naram-ba	Narmer, Abatu	Anjana	Aha	Narmer	Athothis
Shar-gani	Sag-gina	Kunti	Zer-ta	Khent	Kenkenes
Nigigi, Igigi	Bag-gid	Bhagi	Zet-Ata	Tcha	Uenephes
Dudu, Dundu	Dudu, Dunu	Dhundu	Den-Setui	Ten, Semti	Usaphaidos
Full separation from Akkadian rule under Dudu					
No listing	Bi-di	Bahu-Bida	Azab	Atab	Miebidos
No listing	Sheshimmash	Sampati	Smerkhat	Hu	Semempses
Shudur-Kib	Shudur-kib	Shruta	Qa-sen	Qa-sen	Bienekhes

30a. Conquests of Menes: Menes was a man of war and he conquered many lands around Egypt. His seal is found in Crete, and it is not a coincidence that Menes and Minos are both spelled the same in the ancient languages. The Mediterranean Sea was called the Sear of Khar at this time. At the time of Menes' invasion of Crete, the Khar lived there, pirates of the sea. Menes took over the island and the Khar were forced to flee, which they did to Carchemish and Phoenicia. They became mercenaries and mentions of them are known as late as the time of King David when he hired them as guards. Minos I is one and same as Pra Menes. When he took over Crete, he began the Minoan Dynasty of Crete. Both L.Austine Waddell and Immanuel Velikovsky had linked Menes to Minos and back to Manas. Both were called *the Bull man*. It was Minos' wife that was cursed with the white bull that resulted in the Minotaur abomination. Both, Crete and Egypt, had a labyrinth created by Daedalus. Minoan Civilization appeared quite suddenly with copper and bronze without having gone through the Stone Age. Once again the art and burial styles of Crete were the same as both Egypt and Ur of the same time. Both Menes and Minos were Jupiter worshippers. Waddell says that both of them met their death in the land of Erin of Ireland, but Menes died at the fate of a hippopotamus. Menes is said to have invented soft mattresses. Menes' descendents also had Sumerian scripts at Abydos even though they ruled at Agade. The art of Astrology was learned from Cush, but this assumes that Cush is still alive, which is unlikely.

Some ancient documents suggest that Crete was populated by the last of the citizens of Atlantis before it sank into the sea. The ancient document, *Oera Linda Book,* is the source, but it has since been declared a forgery. This book talks about the destruction of Atlantis. It is likely that the destruction of Atlantis (if real) took place during the fall of the tower many years before. Thucydides says it was Minos who invaded Crete the first time (Menes of Agade).

Crete	B.C.	A.T. / B.C.	Crete	B.C.	A.T. / B.C.
Menes / Minos I	1570	2023 / 1942	Lycastus	1362	2234 / 1730
Narmer / Asterius / Atet	N/A	2077 / 1887	Asterius III	1320	2275 / 1689
Cydon	1535	2083 / 1881	Minos III	1300	2294 / 1670
Apteras	1503	2088 / 1876	Deucalion	1239	2354 / 1610
Lapis	1461	2129 / 1835	Catreus	1239	2354 / 1610
Asterius II	1447	2142 / 1822	Idomeneus	1203	2389 / 1575
Minos II	1406	2182 / 1782	Leucus	1183	2408 / 1556
Tectemus	1377	2220 / 1744	Revised adds the son of Menes / Minos		

Timeline of Sargon, Menes, and Abraham:

2001 - 2010 A.T.			2011 - 2020 A.T.			2021 - 2030 A.T.			2031 - 2040 A.T.		
1963 - 1954 B.C.			1953 - 1944 B.C.			1943 - 1934 B.C.			1933 - 1924 B.C		
1	5	9	1	5	9	1	5	9	1	5	9

Noah - 2006

Abraham 2008 A.T. - ...

Zagissi

Sargon at Akkad (Agade)

Sargon in Egypt as Pra

Menes (Manashtushu son of Sargon) at Egypt

Menes/Minos over Crete

31. Bereshit / Genesis 11: Biblical Events of Sargon: Between verse 11:26 and 11:31 well over 130 years passed (Terah went from 70 to 200 years old in this time). Sargon and Menes have both passed and the Babylon / Akkad Empire had passed to the end of Sar-kali reign in Agade and Khent in Egypt. Egypt had revolted completely and was totally sovereign by now, when the area is hit with a huge famine. The Gutium of the Khatti region were now very powerful and making many raids on the Agade Kingdom. The Empire began to disintegrate under Naram-Sin. India and Assyria had started to rebel. The Early Assyrian list ends with Sargon, so his descendents were not able to rule over Assyria. The Guti records the famine (a 12 year drought). This drought was felt as far away as China, leading to the start of the Shang Dynasty there.

The Torah gives no reason for Terah's move out of the land of Ur. Terah's reason for leaving Ur could be two-fold; the famine (as verified by the Midrash) and the increase of invasions by the Guti. The Agade city of Tell-Leilan was deserted and there is no reason for the sudden ghost town. There was no invasion in this village and no major catastrophe that was evident. This city-kingdom was a *major* storehouse for the Agade Kingdom, but with no crops to store, the city became useless. Terah was among vast numbers of migrants leaving the southern area of Agade. Some modern historians believe it was deserted due to a large number of earthquakes, but there is little archaeological evidence of this. The great cities of Mohenjo-Daro and Harappa in the Indus Valley collapsed at the same time.

31a. Brit Bein HaBetarim: Acts 7:1-8 tells how Abraham was called from the *fires of Babylon*, Ur means fire. This call took place 5 years before

Abraham's entry into Canaan. The Jewish Chronology bases the date of the Exodus as having taken place 430 years after this event, not the entry into Canaan. The year of this event is 2078 A.T. or 1886 B.C. The Dead Sea Scrolls, *"Genesis Commentaries"*, confirms this took place when Abraham was 70. The Jewish date for this event is Tishrei 15, 2018 A.M.

Haran is in the area of the Guti or the Khatti. Later we learn that Laban, a relative of Abraham's and descendant of Terah, was a powerful prince in Haran near the Khatti Sea or the Mediterranean Sea. Terah died in Haran at the age of 275 years old. It would appear that the drought was starting to affect the area of Khatti / Guti as well.

31b. The Jews: Modern historians (especially atheistic or non-believing historians) have recently tried to deny the existence of the ancient Jews as having existed, saying that there is no archaeological evidence. Archaeological evidence can be found in Dynasty 19 of Egypt where a stele explicitly indicates that at the time of this stele, Israel was no more.

This revised reconstruction of history shows that not only does history have evidence of the Jews, but that their very existence is based on the Plan of HaShem. The Hyksos period of Egypt is actually the rule of Arabic nations over Egypt. The Hyksos ruled over Egypt for the entire duration of the period of Judges in Israel. This is why Egyptians are never mentioned in the Book of Judges until toward the end when they appear as slaves to the rulers of Egypt (Arabs).

Summary of History before the Jews

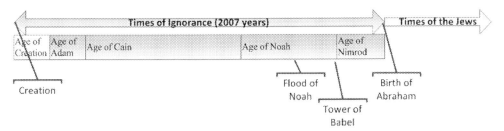

91

Summary of the Jewish Period of History: The Egyptian history and the history of the early Arabs are closely tied to the Jewish history.

			1993 Years					Times of Believers	7	
75	430	430	430	75	70	483		(1993 Years)		Kingdom Age (1000 Years)
	Patriarchs	Judges	Kings				Daniel's 490 years (483 + 7)			
	1290 years of Daniels vision					553		Dispersal of the Jews	7	
	1440 Years									
	1440 + 553 + 7 = 2000 years of the Times of the Jews									
						Times of the Gentiles				
Egyptian Old Kingdom	Egyptian Hyksos Period	Egyptian New Kingdom								
Arabic Nations of Ishmael										

32. Bereshit / Genesis 12: Call of Abraham to Canaan: This follows soon after the death of Terah, even though the verses indicate that Abraham was called from his father's house. The land of Canaan belonged to the Canaanites, who in local history were also called Amorites. Canaan was the one cursed of Noah and thus would lose control over the land according to the curse and become slaves to his kin, which was Terah's line, or Abraham. The Book of Acts reveals that Abraham didn't leave Haran until after his father died. The Hebrew chronologists believe that Abraham left Ur for Canaan and then came back when Terah moved to Haran. The Genesis verses do not confirm their conclusion in that it says *to a land that HaShem would show him*, meaning Abraham had not seen them yet. He arrived in the town of Shechem, the city where Shem was now living as Melchitzedek. The appearance of HaShem was in the form of some kind of vision, and not *in person* as will happen later at the prediction of Isaac.

32a. Date: This date is very important for an accurate dating of history from this point. It has been pointed out that the Jewish chronology dates the Exodus against Brit Bein HaBetarim (in Ur when Abraham was 70). This revised work and that of James Ussher both date the Exodus against this call of Abraham; Nissan 15, 2083 A.T. or April 1881 B.C. James Ussher gives it a year of 2083 A.M. as well as Floyd Nolan Jones and Frank Klassen. David Down and John Ashton give it a year of 1885 B.C. a mere 4 years off from this revised date. Other sources also offer dates for this event:

History Source	Year of this event	History source	Year of this event
Hebrew	2023.7.15 A.M.	James Ussher	2083 A.M.
Julius Africanus	3277 A.M.	Floyd Nolan Jones	2083 A.M.
Book of Jubilees	1951 A.M.	David Down	1875 B.C.
Book of Jasher	2098 A.M.	Frank Klassen	2083 A.M.

By correcting the history through matching with world events, the time of the Patriarchs is exactly 430 years, to the day from the entry into Canaan to the Exodus. This reveals a pattern of history for the Jews of three periods, each 430 years long exactly. While historians would call this an unlikely coincidence, these same historians are the same who would deny the supernatural involvement of HaShem into the history of *His People.*

32b. Famine: The drought had brought on a large famine and many traversed to Egypt, which seemed to be unaffected and had enough to handle the large migration of people seeking to escape hunger and famine in Agade. It would appear that after Abraham established himself in Canaan, he moved on to the Negev toward Egypt.

Zoser or Bagid was the pharaoh in Egypt at the time of the famine. Zoser recorded that the rising of the Nile did not come at its appointed time. Zoser was the pharaoh who mistakenly took Sarai to be his wife and thus bringing down the curse of HaShem on Egypt (not just Zoser). It isn't known how the Pharaoh knew that Abraham was the reason for the plagues visited on Egypt, but he recognized that Abraham was an important man in the eyes of the unknown God. He didn't dare punish Abraham having already seen what would happen just by stealing Abraham's wife. Instead, he loaded Abraham with riches and sent Abraham and his people back to Canaan. The time in Egypt was about 5 years, although no exact time is available. Some extra-Biblical references say he was there as long as 12 years. By the time he returned to Canaan, the land was plush and green again, as indicated by the choice of Lot.

In Agade, the famine over, power moved to Erech (Uruk). They served the moon goddess and resumed many old customs, such as wife immolation. The position of wives was lowered and this attitude of a lower status of women spread to China and Japan (which did not exist as Japan yet). In India, a strong caste system emerged raising priests (Brahmans) to a higher power. The Royal Caste was later eliminated by Purash-Sin. With the Guti invasions, the Babylon Empire started by Cush/Nimrod officially ended.

Zoser's architect Imhotep has been equated to be Joseph, due to the famine story, which in conventional history took place much later than the famine in the first dynasty. Merging the 2 dynasties removes that possibility as Joseph wasn't born for another 200 years. Imhotep was someone of reputation and they built temples to him in conventional dynasty 4. The *Oxyrhynchus* Papyrus relates that King Mycerinus built temples to Imhotep. Imhotep is often the subject of the modern day movies about the *Mummy*. Imhotep and Dzoser are both mentioned together in one relief, it is impossible that they are in different time periods. This revised version rejects the idea that Imhotep is the same Joseph.

33. Bereshit / Genesis 13: Abraham and Lot: Abraham was extremely powerful and wealthy in the land of Canaan. Lot had naturally accumulated as well, just being associated with Abraham in Egypt. They had so much that their respective herdsmen began quarreling. Lot chose the plush land to the East of the Jordon. This separation took place before the covenant of Abraham in 2093 A.T., but there is no exact date.

33a. Dead Sea: The Dead Sea did not exist at the time Lot moved there or before. The 5 cities existed at the edges of what is now the Dead Sea. The *Ebla Tablets* mentions several of the cities, which contradicts modern historians who deny the existence of the 5 cities mentioned in the Bible.

34. Bereshit / Genesis 14: War between Canaan and Babylonians: This war also took place before the covenant of Abraham. Lot is kidnapped as a victim of the war. The war started 14 years before the kidnapping of Lot, who had moved to Sodom. David Rohl believes that the famine that sent Abraham to Egypt caused the unrest between Babylon and Canaanites or Amorites. Rohl quotes *Enuma Anu Enlil: Tablet 20*. "The king of Ur will experience famine. There will be many deaths. The king of Ur will be wronged by his son. Shamash the sun god will catch him. The king's son seized the throne." Amar Sin was not the son due to inherit the throne in Ur.

34a. Battle of Abraham: The Midrash indicates that during the battle, the planet Jupiter was very close to earth (remembering that ancients knew about the moons of Jupiter without a telescope). The closeness lit up the sky at night as if it was day. Tractate Shabbat says that HaShem changed the orbit of Jupiter to show Abraham the uselessness of astrology. It is believed that the closeness of Jupiter caused the Earth to shift the direction of rotation so that Jupiter changed from rising in the East to rising in the West. Changes in the Earth's orbit has been recorded by the Mayans and the Aztecs much later.

Abraham was able to defeat a much larger army with only 318 warriors, the significance of the gematria value of Eliezer, Abraham's servant. Gematria is the study of applying numbers to letters and using the total value to apply another meaning to the word. Melchitzedek is believed to be Shem, the son of Noah, who was still living at this time. Abraham refused to take anything of the spoils because the kings were idolaters and he refused to be associated with them in the eyes of Hashem. He didn't want to owe them anything as well, said right out in the Bible verse 24.

35. Bereshit / Genesis 15:1-21: Covenant of Abraham: This was a vision from HaShem. The promise of HaShem is that an heir from Abraham's own loins will inherit his inheritance. In this promise, HaShem reaffirms that He had appeared to Abraham when Abraham lived in Ur. This supports the verses in Acts where Stephen the Martyr says that HaShem appeared to Abraham in Ur. This covenant is eternal, unlike the covenant of Noah.

35a. Generations of Abraham as strangers: This part promises that for 400 years, Abraham's descendents would be subject to foreign rulers in a strange land, not in Canaan. The Hebrew interpretation is that this 400 year period starts with the birth of Isaac. This revised interpretation is that the time doesn't start until the death of Abraham. From his death until the Exodus, his descendants served Egypt for 330 years (strangers in a foreign land). The last 70 years of the 400 years takes place after Nebuchadnezzar carries them off to Babylon. The 70 years ends when Cyrus decrees that they can return to the land of Israel. The conventional Christian interpretation is that this 400 years starts when Isaac is weaned (about his 5th year), but the Bible/Torah gives no dates for Isaac's weaning.

The promise ends with the words "*but you shall go to your fathers in peace.*" This indicates that nothing in the covenant starts until Abraham dies.

35b. 4th Generation: The return does not refer to the entire 400 years, but to the first enslavement in the 4th generation. This again does not start with Abraham. The enslavement didn't really start in Egypt until the death of Levi. Joshua is the 4th generation from Levi and it was Joshua who led the Israelites into Egypt (Moses was not allowed to do so due to some infraction).

35c. Date of Covenant: This appearance of HaShem came to Abraham in his 85th year, in Nissan 14. Nissan 14, 2093 A.T. or 753134 D.T. Wednesday and March 30, 1871 B.C. 1037780 J.D. Wednesday.

35d. Darkness: The darkness was not a normal darkness but was the terror of the Lord upon him. This terror is not the same as being afraid of wolves. The terror has an inherent peace that only individuals who have experienced it can understand. While you feel terror, you also feel like you want to stay in that terror because underlying that terror is a peace beyond explanation.

36. Bereshit / Genesis 16:1-14: Sarah: Sarah was barren. She couldn't have any kids and they had already been married well over 10 years. The common Christian interpretation is that the Orthodox Jewish belief is that after 10 years, if a wife doesn't bear children, the husband can officially put her away. This revised interpretation does not believe that. The reason being, Rebecca didn't bear Isaac any children for 20 years and there was no indication that Isaac was going to put her away. It is the Jewish interpretation that a wife who cannot bear children within 10 years, is being punished for some sin(s).

36a. Hagar: Having children was all important to Hebrew families, so much so that the husband was often allowed to have sex with other women *without jealousy* so that he had many children. Jacob is a good example. Leah and Rachel were not jealous about Jacob sleeping with the other sister, but they were jealous that the other sister gave more children to Jacob. Hagar conceived and *this made Sarah jealous*. The verses indicate after Hagar got pregnant she began to look down on Sarah. The interpretation is that now that she was having Abraham's son, her status was raised and Abraham and Sarah could no longer treat her as a slave. She became equal to Sarah, which lowered Sarah's status. The Midrash indicates that Hagar was given to Abraham by the Pharaoh and she was formerly an Egyptian princess. Hagar is a play on words and it means *rewarding.* The Pharaoh might have changed her name or added this name to her others as he was rewarding Abraham.

37b. Hagar Flees: Sarah treated Hagar severely forcing Hagar to flee, but an angel told her to go back and submit to the treatment and her son would be blessed. There are 7 men in the full Tanach who were named before birth; Ishmael, Isaac, Moses, Samuel, Solomon, Josiah, and Yeshua Meshach (Jesus the Christ). It was predicted that Ishmael's descendents and Isaac's descendents would be enemies. That plays out today between the Jews and the Muslims. According to the Muslims, Abraham created the shrine called Kaaba or Mecca. The first time the term Arab was used in history was around 835 B.C. Before that they were referred to as Nomads or Ishmaelites or simply Tent dwellers.

37c. Date: Abraham was 86 years old when Ishmael was born in 2094 A.T. This is 1871 B.C.

37d. Islam: Herman Hoeh reports that Kedar was the son of Ishmael by the daughter of Modad. The family of Kedar ruled over the Hejaz for 9 generations. They disappeared but then later reappeared in 122 B.C. They established themselves as the Sherif of Mecca. The English word Sheriff is from this word in Arabic. King Hussein of Modern day Jordon was a direct descendent of this Sherif.

37. Egypt: *Papyrus Prisse* tells us that Sneferu followed right after Huni (of the traditional 3rd Dynasty). It's not known why but modern Egyptologists separated the 4th and 5th Dynasty even though they were of the same family line. Menkauhor of the conventional 5th dynasty starts a new family line. The 5th dynasty moved their pyramids to Abusir. Dr. Breasted's version of the Palermo Stone places Sneferu in the 3rd dynasty. Sneferu lived in the last years of Zoser and had learned how to build pyramids. He built some of the greatest of the pyramids. He is believed to have built the *Bent Pyramid and the Red Pyramid.* Thutmose III of the 18th Dynasty wrote graffiti on the walls of the Bent Pyramid many years later. The Great Sphinx is attributed to the early part of the 4th dynasty. A note by Thutmose IV indicates it was built by Cheops. The Sphinx does not have a beard. Dr. Vassil Dobrev believes that Djedefere built the Sphinx after his father, Khufu.

Conventional Dynasty 4 of Egypt							Rev Dyn 3
Manetho	**Abydos**	**Convention**	**Down / Ashton**	**D /A B.C.**	**David Rohl**	**D.R. B.C.**	**A.T. / B.C.**
Huni							moved
Soris	Sharru	Nebka II	Snerferu	1940	Snerferu	2499	2103 / 1861
Suphis I	Cheops	Cheops	Kufu	1945	Khufu	2475	2116 / 1848
		Djedefre	Djedefre	1870	Djedefre	2452	2138 / 1826
Suphis II	Chephren	Chephren	Khafre	1862	Khafre	2444	2145 / 1819
					Bakare	2419	No listing
Menkheres	Menkaura	Menkaura	Menkaure	1820	Menkaure	2413	2169 / 1795
Rhatoises	Radedf	Sahure					2175 / 1789
Neferirkare (only in revised list from conventional dynasty 5)							2186 / 1778
Bikheris	Shepsekaf	Shepsekaf	Shepseskaf	1800	Shepseskaf	2395	2195 / 1769
Seberkheres					Hardjedef	2389	No listing
Thamfthis							

Conventional Dynasty 5 of Egypt							Rev Dyn 3
Manetho	**Abydos**	**Convention**	**Down / Ashton**	**D /A B.C.**	**David Rohl**	**D.R. B.C.**	**A.T. / B.C.**
Userkheres	Userkaf	Userkaf	Userkaf	1790	Userkaf	2389	
Chephres	Sahura	Sahure	Sahure		Sahure	2382	See above
Neferkheres	Neferakara	Neferirkara	Neferirkare		Neferirkare	2370	See above
Siseres	Shepseskar	Shepsikare	Shepseskar		Shepseskar	2360	See above
Kheres	Neferfra	Nyuserre			Neferefre	2353	2202 / 1762
Rhathures	Raenuser		Raneferer		Niuserre	2350	2204 / 1760
Menkheres	Menkauho	Menkauhor			Menkauhor	2339	2214 / 1750
Tankheres	Dadkara	Djedkare	Djedkare		Izezi	2331	2221 / 1743
Pmnos	Unas	Unas	Unas		Unas	2303	Moved rev 4

Velikovsky points out that the Pyramids are Iron Age products but the traditional dating of the pyramids is long before the Iron Age. He discounts the *metal ages* as a time measuring tool as Iron is easier to make than Bronze but it typically dated after Bronze.

Bimson and Mackay attempt to place Moses at the time of Cheops, but this revised work rejects that claim. They attribute the *Story of Sinuhe* to that of Moses. Djedefere is reputed to have had to clean up Egypt after the death of his father Cheops who left the dynasty in chaos after building so many pyramids from slaves.

The *Palermo Stone* begins listing kings from the Conventional 5th Dynasty. This was the first time that history had recorded names for years, each year having a name. The years soon started to be numbered soon after. The Palermo Stone differs from the Turin Canon in the number of years that kings ruled. The Palermo Stone does tell us that Horus or Hor was the main deity of this time. This refutes the claim of modern historians that Osiris and Ra were worshipped in the early years of Egypt. The Apis Bull is mentioned as well in the Palermo Stone. The worship of the sun didn't start until late in the 5th dynasty. This is the first mention of *Re or Ra*.

Dr. Breasted mentions that a single man, *Ptahshepses*, lived from the time of Menkare (4th Dynasty), until Niuserre (5th dynasty), meaning that the kings between them all lived in the lifetime of this man. That's only 45 years. David Rohl indicates that this might be as much as 75 years.

38. Bereshit / Genesis 17:1-27: The Covenant of Abraham: HaShem appeared to Abraham, a descent of HaShem. This descent is twofold; for Abraham's covenant and to deal with the sin of the Sodom Plain. This is the first time that HaShem reveals Himself as El Shaddai *"God Almighty"*. Abraham and Sarah both got name changes here. This Age is arbitrarily named the Age of Promise as Isaac was the promised child of Abraham. Isaac is a strong arche-type of Yeshua HaMaschiach (Jesus) and so not only is the promise about Isaac but a strong prediction of the Savior.

38a. Date: Abraham is 99 years old meaning that this event fell on Nissan 10, 2107 A.T. or 758170 D.T. and March 30, 1857 B.C., 1042893 J.D. a Saturday. The orthodox Jewish chronology from the Midrash places this event on Tishrei 10, 2047 A.M. but they fail to take into account that HaShem said He would return in the same season. The birth of Isaac is in the spring, not the fall. James Ussher, Floyd Nolan Jones, and Frank Klassen all put this event in 2107 A.M.

38b. Abraham's Covenant: As soon as Abraham knew who was there with him, he *threw* himself prostrate on his face in humility before HaShem. This was no slow easy kneeling down on his knees or bowing of the head. He *threw* himself to the ground. The sign of the covenant is circumcision. The covenant was confirmed by HaShem to be through Isaac, not Ishmael. Ishmael was 13 when he was circumcised. Isaiah 53:10

indicates that if you believe in the Messiah (before He lived or after), you became a member of Abraham's descendents, even if you didn't have a direct blood line. The covenant is not just between Abraham, but between Abraham and his descendents and all *believers of the Messiah*. Sarah didn't get pregnant right away as she had Isaac a year later in the same month as the visit with HaShem. When HaShem returned the next year, Sarah made *Ugoth*, which is unleavened bread, a bread used during the Feast of Unleavened Bread in Nissan (spring).

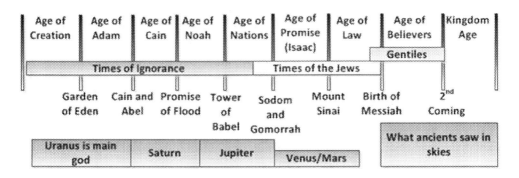

39. Bereshit / Genesis 18:1-33: Promise of Isaac next year: Abraham recognized the three men immediately and again bowed down before them. This time, Abraham offers them a meal, which consisted of unleavened bread, the formal type of bread given at the Feast of Unleavened Bread in the month of Nissan (spring). HaShem received their offering. The statement was made by HaShem that nothing is impossible for HaShem. He also says that Abraham had been singled out for the blessing of the nations. Abraham deals with HaShem for the sake of his nephew Lot. He didn't want his nephew and his nephew's family to suffer for the sins of Gomorrah. This descent is for the sins of Sodom and Gomorrah introducing the next age.

CHAPTER 7

AGE OF PROMISE

40. Bereshit / Genesis 19:1 – 20:18: Destruction of Sodom and Gomorrah: Like Abraham, Lot too recognized the visitors as angels of the Lord. HaShem was no longer with the two angels. This event took place on the 15th of Nissan. The visit of the angels took an entire day. The citizens of the town attacked at dusk which was the 16th of Nissan. As his guests, Lot was responsible for the safety of the guests by custom. He offered his two virgin daughters in place of the angels. It was Lot's reputation that had saved the virginity of his daughters in the first place as the town respected Abraham's and Lot's significant role in the area of Canaan. Four people were urged to flee, but Lot's wife turned back and became a pillar of salt. Ginzberg believes that *Irith* turned back and saw the Shekinah Glory and was turned by the sight. Josephus reports that her pillar could still be seen in his day (70 A.D.). Velikovsky reports that the event was the result of the comet Typhon which was later Venus. There have been other reports of humans being turned instantly into salt, one in Chile. In Egypt, Typhon was considered an evil god.

Moab	B.C.	Moab	B.C.
Lot	1857	Mizpeh I	1100
Moab	1837	Kemosh 1	1075
Unknown		Mizpeh II	1050
Zippor	1215	Ariel	975
Balak	1190	Kemosh II	950
Baal-Paor	1165	Kemosh III	875
Eglom	1140	Mesha	825

Lot went to Tzoar and stayed in the mountains. His two daughters thought the entire world had been destroyed and they were the last humans alive. While he was their father, the command to procreate the earth took priority so they both lay with him in two nights. They both had sons later that year. Moab was one of the two sons born and the following is an estimated list of Moab kings.

40a. Dead Sea: Archaeology has revealed the remains of villages at the edges of the Dead Sea. The Dead Sea was created at this event, the destruction of the 5 towns in the plain. The Dead Sea is a salt sea and does not support any life. The Dead Sea curse upon the sins of the area is the same as the curse of the earth when Adam sinned. The land was cursed to never be a plush plain again, but rather a dead area.

40b. Famine: This famine was local to the area of Canaan. A month later, Abraham moved to the land of the Philistines due to the famine. The Philistines were fairly new to the area, probably related to the Carians that had deserted Crete when Menes/Minos invaded Crete. Abraham remained there for 26 years. Isaac was born there. Abimelech was a title, not a name. It means father/king (Abi = father, melech = king). Sarah conceived shortly after arriving in the land.

Abraham uses the same tactic in Philistine as he did in Egypt by declaring Sarah as his sister. He didn't lie. Sarah was his half-sister through another mother. The question is why he did this. He was a powerful man in the area, one of reputation. He had demonstrated powerful war tactics when he defeated the 5 kings of Babylon. HaShem once again intervenes and tells Abimelech that he is to die because he took a married woman. Abimelech had not yet taken her sexually so the dream served more as a warning. Abraham is declared in the dream to Abimelech to be a prophet. Once again, Abraham's riches are advanced by Abimelech. The curse placed on the house of Abimelech was the hold on every womb of every woman. In order to know this curse, it took time to realize that no women were getting pregnant and yet, Sarah conceived by Abraham as promised by HaShem. It would appear that all of this took a few months since Sarah would have been pregnant and Abimelech would have seen that. The other possibility is that all of this took place after the birth of Isaac but that also seems unlikely. Abimelech would have known that Isaac was Sarah's son.

41. Bereshit / Genesis 21:1-21: Isaac: Just as HaShem visited the Virgin Mary, He visited Sarah and while Isaac was not the child of HaShem as Yeshua was, Isaac was the child of promise. Isaac was born in the same season as the visit of HaShem the previous year.

41a. Dates: Abraham is declared to be 100 years old, which places the birth in the year 2108 A.T. The exact date would be Nissan 14, 2108 A.T. or 758534 D.T. (Saturday). The equivalent Gregorian date would be April 4, 1856 B.C., or 1043264 J.D. Saturday. The *Book of Jubilees* places his birth in the month of Tsivan (4ᵗʰ month). The Jewish chronology gives Nissan 14, 2048 A.M. James Ussher and the Hebrew chronology both state that Isaac was weaned at the age of 5 in 2113 A.M. (by Ussher's dating). This is the year used by Ussher to determine the date of the Exodus, 400 years later to this year. The Bible mentions the weaning, but does not give an exact date for it, so this is rejected by this revised history. HaShem is an exact God and would not leave such things open to question.

41b. Hagar and Ishmael: Since Sarah had a son of her own, and Ishmael was older, she had Hager and Ishmael removed so that Ishmael would not be the heir of Abraham's fortunes. After the encounter with the angel, Hagar and Ishmael went to live in the area of Paran. Hagar lost her marriage rights and Ishmael lost his first born rights. This is the one of the reasons for the war between the Arabs (Muslims) and the Jews. In the Koran, there is no mention of Hagar or of Ishmael. All references to these two are from secondary sources. There is a prayer mentioned in the Koran that does reference Ishmael. Supported in the Koran is when Abraham takes Keturah and she bore him 6 sons. The Koran does not offer proof that Ishmael was sent away. The Muslims do take the Jewish version and believe that Abraham took Ishmael and Hagar to Mecca, Kaaba. Later in the sacrifice of Isaac, the Muslims believe that it was Ishmael that was sacrificed, not Isaac. *Eid al-Adha* is the Muslim festival that celebrates the sacrifice of Abraham's son.

Sneferu was the Pharaoh of Egypt according to this revised dating. There is no record that Sneferu ever invaded Canaan, which supports the Biblical narrative of seeing no invasions from Egypt. Sneferu concentrated his efforts on Africa. His invasions are recorded on the Palermo Stone. It is believed that Hagar found a wife for Ishmael in Egypt.

41c. Isaac as Type: This work has been careful about trying to apply types as they can be overdone by zealous Christians who want to make everything figurative and make the Bible into a *mysterious narrative.* This work believes that typology is used by HaShem to *reveal, not to hide.* Isaac is such a strong type of Yeshua that it would be a crime to not mention Isaac as a type of Yeshua, particularly when he not only typifies the Christ, but lends certain predictions about the coming Messiah. In this case, the typology of Isaac once again reveals that HaShem is not a God of secrets, but wishes to reveal to us what He will do and what He has done! Isaac has already been noted as a *Child of Promise* just as the Messiah was. Hebrews 10:1 says that *types are the shadows of good things to come and the very image of the thing.*

If Ishmael plays into the types, Ishmael would by a type of Adam, HaShem's *first son,* and Isaac, HaShem's *second son and the favored.* This plays out again with Esau and Jacob. Ishmael and Esau both rejected what was given to them as his birthright just as Adam rejected his in the Garden of Eden. Esau was a red man just as Adam was a red man.

Isaac	Yeshua Messiah (Jesus the Christ)
The first born of his mother	The first born of Mary
Was promised by HaShem directly	Was promised through Gabriel, messenger
Was named before he was born	Mary was given His name before birth
Was "sacrificed" at the age of 37	Crucified at the age of 37
Was dead to his father for 3 days	Was in the grave for 3 days
Accompanied by 2 other men (servants)	Crucified by two other men (thieves)
Rode an ass to the mountain	Rode an ass into Jerusalem
Carried his own wood to the alter	Carried His own cross to the hill
A substitute ram was supplied	Was the ram for sacrifice for all sins
Ram was found in thorn bush	Wore a crown of thorns

Lived after being sacrificed	Lived after rising again from the dead.
Messenger was sent to fetch his bride	Holy Spirit was messenger to fetch bride
Met his bride halfway across the field	Will meet his bride in the skies, halfway
He inherited his father's kingdom	Will rule his father's kingdom.

41d. Assyria: With the end of the Sargon Empire, Assyria begins to gain power. Assyria did not keep accurate records and there are three known different versions of the Eponym List of Assyria. The Assyrians are moon and Dagan worshippers, sexually predominate gods. Ishme-Dagan was the name of one of the Isin rulers, as they often took the name of their god at the end of their name. Sin was the name of the moon god and many names end in Sin (not to be confused with the English term of the same spelling).

The following list starts just shortly after Sargon died and is the first original Eponym List. At this time, they were still subject to Isin, but their independence is not far away. The revised dates (A.T. / B.C.) are *best guess estimates* based on archaeological records which are few and far between for this area and time. Naram Sin is most likely the son of Menes, who ruled over Babylon after the death of his grandfather, Sargon. His dates are based on the rules of Sargon and Menes. The time difference between Naram and Assur Dugal indicates that there were probably other rulers over the area between them as it is unlikely that 3 rulers ruled for almost 400 years.

Assyria	J.J. G.	Hoeh	Roux	A.T. / B.C.
Puzur Ashur II				
Naram-Sin				2077 / 1887 ??
Erishum II				
Shamshi Adad I				
Ishme Dagan	40 years			
Assur Dugal		1179-1173		2458 / 1506
Nasir Sin	6 sons			
Belu-bani	10 yrs	1173-1163		2465 / 1499
Libaja	17	1163-1146		2475 / 1489
Sarma-Adad	12	1146-1134		2492 / 1472

Iptar Sin	12	1134-1122		2504 / 1460	
Bazaja	28	1122-1094		2516 / 1448	
Lullaja	6	1094-1088	1621	2544 / 1420	
Su-Ninua	14	1088-1074	1615	2550 / 1414	
Sarma Adad	3	1074-1071	1601	2573 / 1391	
Erishum III	13	1071-1058		2575 / 1389	
Shamshi Adad II	6	1058-1052		2577 / 1377	
Ishme-Dagan II	16	1052-1036		2582 / 1372	
Shamshi Adad III	16	1036-1020		2597 / 1357	
Assur Nirari I	26	1020-994	1547	2622 / 1342	
Puzur Asshur III	14	994-980	1521	2647 / 1317	
Enlil Nasir I	13	980-967		2660 / 1304	
Nur Ili ben Enlil	12	967-955		2672 / 1292	
Asshur Saduni	1 mon	955		2683 / 1281	
Assur Rabi I	ousted	--			
Assur Nadine	4	955-930		2683 / 1281	
Enlil Nasir II	6	--	1420	2686 / 1278	
Start of Assyrian Eponym List					

42. Bereshit / Genesis 22-23: Akedah – Sacrifice of Isaac: Abraham is commanded to sacrifice his only son, Isaac, since Ishmael had been sent away many years earlier. He was ordered to sacrifice his *favored* son, whom he loved. This is an extreme typological resemblance of Yeshua who was HaShem's favored Son, whom He loved. The trip took 3 days to get to the mountain of sacrifice. This also was typical of Yeshua, who was chosen on the 10th of Nissan, the day He entered Jerusalem on an ass, the same as Isaac rode an ass with his father to the mountain. There were two servants that went along, like the two thieves who died alongside of Yeshua. Isaac also rode an ass to his own crucifixion. Between the 11th and 13th was three days, the amount of time the trip took to *see the place afar*. The three days could also represent the 3 days that Yeshua was in the grave. On the 14th of Nissan, Isaac carried his own wood, the same as Yeshua being forced to carry His own cross. The time of this event took place when Isaac was 37 years old. Many Sunday school teachers imply that he was just a boy, but Isaac was anything but. This is the same age as Yeshua when He was crucified. All of these details were predictive of what HaShem planned and is revealing to us. II Chronicles' points out that Mount Moriah would be the future place of the Temple of Solomon, and Yeshua's place of trial for His crucifixion.

Unlike Yeshua, Isaac was not really killed but was replaced by a ram, the guilt ram sacrifice for our sins, who was found in a bush of thorns, like the crown of thorns placed on the head of Yeshua before being raised up over the earth. Isaiah 53:7 indicates that Yeshua didn't say a word. Isaac did not object to being sacrificed by his father and he was definitely old enough to do so. They both went willingly!

The Koran indicates that it was Ishmael who was sacrificed, rather than Isaac.

42a. Dates: *The Book of Jubilees* indicates that it was the demon Mastema who enticed Abraham to sacrifice Isaac. The date of the Akedah according to Jubilees is 2003 A.M. Louis Ginzberg agrees that a demon enticed Abraham. The *Book of Jasher* places this event in 2144 A.M. James Ussher and Josephus places this event in 2133 A.M. This revised work places this event on Nissan 14, 2145 A.T. 771854 D.T. (Friday). The equivalent Gregorian year is 1819 B.C. The Jewish Chronology places this event in 2084 A.M.

42b. Sarah: Abraham stayed in Kiriath-Arba, City of Four and hears about his brother's family. Isaac went back to his mother who died later this same year at the age of 127. She is the only woman in the Bible whose age is declared at the age of her birth, confirming that she was 10 years younger than Abraham who was 137. Abraham, Sarah, Isaac, and Rebekah are all buried in a cave in this city. Some believe that she died upon hearing that Isaac was still alive, from the shock.

Ginzberg believes that Lot and Abimelech died about the same time as Sarah. Sarah's grave was purchased from the Hittites of Haran (Heth). Laban, a relative of Abraham lived in this area. The Talmud indicates that this was about the time of the testing of Job as well. Nahor II also died about this time according to the Hebrew chronology. Abraham paid 400 shekels of silver for the cave. The average yearly salary at this time was about 8 shekels of silver. The 400 shekels could be representative of the 400 years that Israel would serve other rulers (the prediction of HaShem to Abraham).

43. Bereshit / Genesis 24: Isaac marries: The messenger is never named, but it is believed to be Eliezer. This revised version does not believe that it was Eliezer. Why wouldn't HaShem use his name as Eliezer had already been named in former scriptures? The Hebrew chronology believes it is Eliezer. The placing of the hand under the thigh is called the *Dread Oath.* If the servant failed and it was not his fault, he is released, but if he failed and it was his fault, he would be killed. Fail or succeed, Isaac was not to be taken to Haran. The messenger turned his fate over to HaShem at the well and HaShem answered him immediately!

The Midrash states that Bethuel had died and Laban his son, was now the patriarch of the family. Laban is mentioned on an Assyrian stone that also tells the area of Laban accurately. Laban was an opportunist and saw a way to marry his family with that of an already powerful patriarch (Abraham). Rebekah could not be given away without her own permission, since her father was dead. Isaac met her halfway across the field as she arrived near his place of residence. Isaac takes her back to his mother's tent. He had been mourning for the 3 years since her death. He was 40 when Rebekah became his wife. Rebekah was no meek woman. She was able to draw large amounts of water for him and for his camel.

43a. Types: It has already been stated that Isaac is a strong archetype of Yeshua Messiah. Rebekah becomes an archetype for the Bride of the Messiah, or *the church*. This messenger (Holy Shekinah Glory or Holy Spirit) follows closely with that typology. Once Yeshua goes to heaven to take His role as our High Priest in heaven, the messenger, *the Shekinah Glory*, is sent to earth to retrieve the bride that is to go to meet the Savior at the end of the 6th day (6000 years). The messenger brought Sarah back on a camel, which has one mark of cleanness and one mark of uncleanness, representing her two sons, one unclean (Esau) and one clean (Jacob). She met Isaac halfway across the field. It is believed here that when Yeshua descends in the clouds, that the bride, (true believers in Yeshua Messiah) will rise up and meet him in the sky, halfway.

One important note is that the servant's success was not his own. We often wish to believe that our success is by our own hard work and cleverness. It is HaShem who decides who shall succeed.

43b. Dates: Abraham was 140 years old when Isaac married Rebekah. The year is 2148 A.T. or 1816 B.C. The Jewish chronology places this event in the year 2087 A.M. The *Book of Jubilee* places this event in the 2020 A.M. James Ussher gives it a year of 1856 B.C.

44. Bereshit / Genesis 25: Abraham marries again: This event took place *after* the marriage of Isaac (and death of Sarah), but it is not known how long after. Abraham married Keturah. The Jewish chronology believes that this was Hagar under a new name. Hagar would have been around 70 + years at this time, so this revised chronicle does not believe it was Hagar. Keturah bore Abraham 6 more sons. To keep his inheritance of Canaan going to Isaac, Abraham sent the sons away when they were of age. Abraham had 8 sons all together.

    44a Epher ben Midian: The Midianites were direct descendents of Abraham. Epher is believed by Josephus, *Antiquities*, to have joined up with a Greek hero by the name of Hercules and they defeated Libya. Alexander Polyhistor agrees with Josephus. Hercules married one of Epher's daughters and had a son, Diodorus. Africa is believed to have been named after Epher. Hercules is the progenitor of the Dorians who later invaded Greece. Josephus believes that Epher was known as Atlas, one of the strong men of Hercules' group. The traditional Herakles is reputed to have lived at the end of the Argive Period of Greece around 1250 B.C., some 600 years later.

    44b. Isin: The rise of the Mar-Tu (Amorites in Canaan) to the west was causing havoc. The roving bands of desert dwellers raided villages of Shu-Shin of Ur. With the rise of Ibbi-Sin in Ur, the Ur dynasty crumbled. Ibbi was captured and taken prisoner. This has been confirmed in the *Isin-Nippur Chronicles*. Alongside the Isin Dynasty was the Larsa Dynasty. They were constantly at war, but never managed to defeat each other.

Isin Dynasty: This ends the SKL and begins the Assyrian Eponym List. Elamite names are supplied by Professor Scheil. Ishme-Dagan is listed in Assyria II without a revised date. G.R. = George Roux; D.R. = David Rohl.

SKL / IKL	Assyria	Elam	India AKL	G.R.	D.R.
Ishi-irra / Bi-ash	Ushpia	Ushia Bi-gal	Vishva-saha	2017	1805
Su-ilisu			Khat-vanga	1984	1772
Iddin-Dagan		Shu-truk-ask	Dhirgha-bahu	1974	1752
Ishme-Dagan		Kutir-ash	Raghu	1953	1731
Lipit-Ishtar		Lila-ir-tash	Aja	1934	1711
Original dynasty ends here. This begins the Amorite Dynasty of Isin					
Ur-Ninurta	Dag-shi-ash		Dasha-ratha	1923	1700
Bur-Sin			Rama Chandra	1895	1672
Lipit-Enlil			Kusha-Lava	1873	1651
Irra-imitti	Ititi	Simti/Shilhak	Atitha	1868	1646
Enlil-bani	Gaba-ni-pi		Nishada	1860	1638
Zambija			Nala		1614
Iter-pisa					1611
Urdukuga				1836	1607
Sin-magir		Kudur-ma-piug	Nabha	1827	1603
Damiq-ilisu			Pundarika	1816	1592

The Isin adopted the Creation and Flood stories of the Bible. The founder of this dynasty was an Elamite or Persian. Larsa was just a local dynasty without any real power.

44c. China/India: China and India began to separate from the western rulers. Rama Chandra is famous in Indian documentation, *Ramayanna, Adventures of Rama*.

44d. Ishmaelites: These descendents of Ishmael lived in the area between Egypt and Canaan, in what is now the Gaza Strip. Ishmael died at the age of 137.

44e. Shem ben Noah: Shem died when Abraham was 150 years of age, in 2158 A.T. or 1806 B.C. He had seen the rise of civilization, the fall of the tower of Babel, the confusion of the languages and the rise and fall of the First Babylonian Empire. It is likely that he was personally involved in the transference of the knowledge of the events of the Flood directly to Abraham.

45. Bereshit / Genesis 25:19-34: Jacob and Esau: Isaac is 60 years old when Rebekah has Esau and Jacob. This is an example where a wife was not able to bear children for 20 years, as Isaac was 40 when they got married.

There is no sign that Isaac considered putting Rebekah away, according to the 10 year rule. Esau was a hunter and Jacob was a sheepherder. Esau was the first of the twins to come out and so the birthright was his as the older son. However, when Esau was hungry, he sold his birthright to Jacob. Esau despised his birthright by selling it off so easily. Abraham died about the same time that Esau sold his birthright. Esau is the progenitor of the Edomites.

45a. Date: The revised date of their birth is 2168 A.T. or 1796 B.C. The Hebrew chronology places this in 2108 A.M. James Ussher places the Flood of Ogyges at this time but this narrative believes this took place much later during the time of Moses.

45b. Famine: There was a new local famine, *aside from the previous famine that had occurred in the days of Abraham.* Isaac went to Abimelech, probably the son of the Abimelech of Abraham. Isaac was told by HaShem not to go down to Egypt, but stay in the Philistines. For some reason, Isaac does the same thing that Abraham did in declaring his wife as his sister. This is why it is believed here that this isn't the same Abimelech since the original would have suspected the same ruse. The event of the original Abraham to Abimelech took place over 60 years ago. The Philistines had stopped up the wells dug by Abraham years ago. Now they argued over the same wells.

45c. Types: Just as Isaac was a strong type of Yeshua, the two sons represent two types of people that will result from the new Christian Order of Yeshua. Esau represents the wicked thief and Jacob the thief that accepted Yeshua. This is the new definition of all peoples, whether they believe on Jesus as Savior or not.

46. Bereshit / Genesis 26:34-35: Esau marries: Esau married outside of the family, taking Hittites women to wife. Esau was 40 years old making this the year 2208 A.T. 1756 B.C. Ishmael died in 2231 A.T. Marrying the Hittite wives took place without Isaac's approval. It is easy to see that Esau realized that after Jacob brought home a wife from the house of Laban.

47. Bereshit / Genesis 27: Flight of Jacob: Jacob steals Esau's blessing. Some issues had come about due to the fact that Jacob *stole* the blessing by deception. Isaac wanted his firstborn to have parental merit to justify the blessing, thus the request for stew. Rebekah understood that the Jacob was to be the blessed son through some insight and Jacob was her favorite. After the mistake was made, Jacob too, realized it was HaShem's control that made this happen. It was Rebekah's idea and she took the responsibility for it but Jacob was not a young child. His decision to go along had to be from some insight of his own. However, at one point Jacob tells Isaac that he is Esau, which was an outright lie. Even still, once the blessing was given, it could not be given to Esau. Jacob received the blessing of Abraham. Anyone who cursed Jacob would be cursed. He even told Esau that once blessed, Jacob could not be unblessed. Esau is angry enough to want to kill Jacob, so Rebekah sent him away to her brother, Laban. Ginzberg believes that Rebekah got word about her brother's daughters when he was 56.

One of the records of Assur-Nirari ben Isme-Dagan of one of the Assyrian Eponym lists records that he set up a Stele in the *great country of Laban on the shore of the Great Sea (Mediterranean Sea)*. He is traditionally dated around 1500 B.C. By this revised dating, he has not yet started to rule over the Isin Dynasty. This verifies that Laban was not just a local family, but a chieftain of strong reputation.

47a. Date: The date is calculated backwards from a statement later in Genesis, when Jacob stands before the Pharaoh during the famine of Joseph.

- Jacob is 130 at entry to Egypt when he stands before the Pharaoh.
- Joseph is 39 at the same time, although he would turn 40 at the end of the year.
- Jacob was 91 in the year of the birth of Joseph.
- Jacob served Laban 14 years when Joseph was born at the end of the 14 years.
- Jacob was 77 years old at the beginning of his service to Laban, which is the year given in this revised chronology.

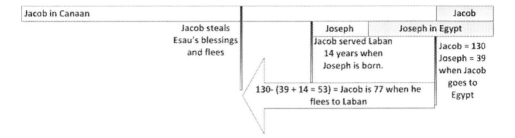

The revised date is Nissan 10, 2245 A.T. 807850 D.T. Sunday, or March 27, 1719 B.C. 1093294 J.D. The Jewish chronology places this event in 2171 A.M. The Midrash places it in 2173 A.M. The Book of Jubilees places this date in 2114 A.M. Jacob is 77 years old.

47b. Esau: He realized having chosen a wife from the Hittites was a mistake, so he turns to the daughters of Ishmael.

48. Bereshit / Genesis 28:10-22: Jacob's Travels: Jacob uses a stone for a pillow and has a dream about angels ascending and descending on a ladder. HaShem appears to Jacob in this dream and declares Himself to be the God of Abraham and the God of Isaac. The blessing given to Isaac and Abraham is given to Jacob. Jacob is promised that Jacob will return to this land. Jacob names the site Bethel (later to be Bethlehem). Before it was named Luz. Bethel means *House of God*. HaShem is not only Jacob's God, but his *Shomer, Guardian.*

48a. Date of Dream: Nissan 14, 2245 A.T. 807854 D.T. Wednesday or April 1, 1719 B.C. 1093298 Wednesday.

49. Bereshit / Genesis 29: Jacob works for Laban: Jacob comes across the women of the town of Laban who were tending the sheep flocks. Rachel, daughter of Laban, appears with her flocks. The stone covering the well was large but Jacob was stronger than most men and he moved the stone away by himself. He then introduces himself to Rachel as the son of her aunt. Jacob begins to serve 7 years for Rachel. Of Jacob's sons, the only year of birth that is known is that of Joseph. The others have some question attached to them. The question arises is are the 12 patriarchs all born in the 2nd 7 year period or were they scattered over the 1st 14 years. Below are the schemas for both possibilities:

It is clear from verse 20 that Jacob served for 7 years *before he got Rachel but was tricked to take Leah.* The revised stance is that all 12 were born in 1 seven year period from 2252 to 2258 A.T. Joseph was the last and was born in the 12th month of the year 2258 A.T.

The first is the schema for the 14 years of birth for the patriarchs:

Year	Leah	Rachel	Bilhah	Zilpah
2245 A.T.	Reuben			
2246 A.T.	Simeon			
2247 A.T.	Levi			
2248 A.T.				
2249 A.T.	Judah		Dan	
2250 A.T.			Naphtali	
2251 A.T.				Gad
2252 A.T.				Asher
2253 A.T.				
2254 A.T.	Issachar			
2255 A.T.				
2256 A.T.	Zebulun			
2257 A.T.	Dinah (sister)			
2258 A.T.		Joseph		

This is the schema for all of them being born in the 2nd 7 year period.

Month	2252 A.T.	2253	2254	2255	2256	2257	2258
1 Nissan						Asher Birth	Leah Clean
2 Iyyar	Reuben Conc				Naph Birth	Issachar Birth Zilpah Clean	Dinah and Joseph both conc

3 Tsivan				Judah Birth Gad Birth	Bilhah Clean	Leah Clean	
4 Tammuz				Leah Clean Dan Birth	Zilpah Clean	Zebulun Conc	
5 Av			Levi Birth	Bilhah Clean	Asher Conc		
6 Elul			Leah Clean	Naphtali Conc	Issachar Conc		
7 Tishrei		Simeon Birth	Judah Conc	Gad Conc			
8 Marcheshvan		Lean Clean	Dan Conc				
9 Kislev	Reuben Birth	Levi Conc					
10 Teves	Leah Clean Month						
11 Shevat	Simeon Conc						
12 Adar						Zebulun Birth	Dinah and Joseph Birth

Having them born in a 14 year period does give greater clarity to the story of Judah and Tamar which has to be squeezed into 7 less years. Counting the years of the story of Judah and Tamar, it is hard to conceive that this story fits into the birth of Reuben to the Entry into Egypt by Jacob. By these revised dates, Reuben would be only 5 years old when Rachel took his mandrakes. Not only does the conception and 9 months have to be taken into account, but also 40 days of cleansing for each mother before they could get pregnant again; a total of 10 months and 10 days. However, Genesis 29:25 clearly says: *"did I not serve thee for Rachel?"* meaning that he had already served 7 years when he was given Leah to wife. A week later, Rachel was also given to him, so that in the next 7 years, the 2 wives and their handmaidens would produce sons for Jacob.

The exact births of the patriarch's is not necessarily relevant to the overall Plan of HaShem except for the birth of Joseph, which is the same in either schema. This shouldn't be an important issue of debate, as if HaShem wanted us to know exactly, He would have told us.

49a. Babylon Empire II: During his time in Haran in the area of the Hittites, Babylon had become an empire again. Larsa and Babylon are matched to be at the same time by a document that links Sumuabum, the Amorite, and Sumu-el of Larsa. Babylon invaded Larsa and created a new capital, BAbl-ilani(Bab-ili or Babel), which in Sumerian means *Gates of the gods*. This implies that the Babylon that we have talked about didn't truly become Babylon until now. This goes back to the revised supposition that Kish was the original Babylon talked about in the Bible. By the time Moses wrote the Pentateuch, the area was known by *Babylon* and is so referred for that reason as Babylon. Khammurabi's father captured Isin in his 17th year. The names of the kings in the list have to be matched by meaning, not phonetically, but the lists match perfectly between the dynasties.

Name	Finegan	Rohl	Roux	Rev A.T. B.C	Match with other rulers
Sumuabum	14 yrs	1667	1894	2245 / 1719	Chiung of China and Unas of Egypt, Sumuabum is the nephew of Rama Chandra of India
Sumulael	36 yrs	1653	1880	2258 / 1706	Joseph / Eratus of Sicyon
Sabium	14 yrs	1617	1844	2293 / 1671	Teti of Egypt / Shang Dynasty
Apil-Sin	18 yrs	1603	1830	2306 / 1658	Bela of Edom
Sin-muballit	20 yrs	1585	1812	2323 / 1641	Pepi
Hammurabi	43 yrs	1565	1792	2342 / 1622	Duecalion of Crete / Spartus
Samsuiluna	38 yrs	1522	1749	2384 / 1580	Myceneus of Sparta
Abjeshuh	28 yrs	1484	1711	2421 / 1543	Moses / Ishme Dagain

Ammiditana	37 yrs	1456	1683	2448 / 1516	Marathus of Sicyon
Ammisaduga	21 yrs	1419	1646	2484 / 1480	Chung Ting of China
Samsuditana	31 yrs	1398	1625	2504 / 1460	Corax of Sicyon
Agum II of Hittites		1362	1595		

49b. Venus: Scientists and historians have maintained that our solar system is millions of years old and has not changed in all that time. Yet, archaeology has supplied us with proof that this is not true. The Venus Tablets of Ammisaduga (valid archaeological stone tables) show that Venus was a comet in his lifetime (British Museum K3032). The tablets were found by Sir Austin Henry Layard. David Rohl believes that the tablets were done during 21 years of Ammisaduga's rule. The orbital path that the tablets suggest is a far cry from the current orbit of Venus. As per status quo, error is assigned to the tablets, but the math is too accurate for the tablets to be in error. That and the fact that another set of tablets, *Hindu Tablets*, validate the Babylonian tablets perfectly.

49c. Egypt: The last ruler of the traditional dynasty 5 is Unas. Dodson believes he is the father of Teti, the official start of dynasty 6. Unas came to power under mysterious circumstances. He moved to the south part of the Nile (referred to as Upper Nile as it runs north). The Abydos List for this dynasty is lost or never existed. Two different inscriptions of Pepi refer to invasions he made against the *Asiatics* (Bedouin Arabs). They are usually attributed to two different Pepi's, but the revised interpretation is that they both belong to one Pepi.

This revised version believes that dynasty 12 and dynasty 6 are the same dynasty. Because names differ for the same person in different areas, the two dynasties were kept separate. The basis for this revised belief is given in great detail in other works: *Revised History of the Ancient World by Anthony Lyle.* It is under Pepi that Joseph ben Jacob lived. It was during Pepi's rule that the great famine of Joseph took place. At this point, the dynasty is just starting.

Dynasty 6	Dynasty 12	Vizier	Notes	AT/BC
Unas				2248 / 1716
Teti I	Amenemhet I	Joseph /	Famine in 20th year.	2276 / 1688
Pepi	Sesostris	Mentuhotep	Both ruled 90 years.	2327 / 1637
Nemtyemsaf	Amenemhet 4	Mentuhotep II	Both killed before father	2417 / 1547
Nitocris	Sobeknefru	Mentuhotep III	Both ruled less than a year	2422 / 1542
Pepi did not die until the year that Niocris ruled. His son died before him.				

A match with the 20th year of Amenehet I ties directly to Joseph and creates a direct date match between the two dynasties and Joseph.

49d. Leah's first sons: The schema above shows that the first sons born all to Leah. Each of the sons are reputed to have written testaments upon the nearness of death. Unfortunately, most of them were doctored by "do-gooder" Christians in the first century A.D. to *correct* their dates. This makes the testaments unreliable. According to Levi, he was around 20 when the rape of Dinah took place. The Testament of Judah indicates that there were many wars between the Assyrians and the Amorites (what the family of Isaac and Jacob was referred to).

50. Bereshit / Genesis 30: Patriarchs: It has already been pointed out that giving children to a husband was the most important. A man could have sex with another woman, but if that other woman had a child than THAT became the point of contention between the two women. In this case, Leah had 4 sons and Rachel had none. The concern for Rachel was that she had sinned and HaShem had closed her womb. Rachel even accuses Jacob of not giving her children. Using the same method as Sarah (with Hagar), Rachel decided to have children through a surrogate, her handmaid. When Leah saw Rachel's success, she did the same with her own handmaid. The next 4 sons were all born through handmaids. It became a contest to win Jacob's love by giving him more children. Who he had sex with to have those children was irrelevant. This was the mindset of that time. It was the same mindset in many other cultures of that time as well. Lady Ash, wife of Sargon, was never concerned about his concubines.

The Testament of Naphtali indicates that Rachel deceived Jacob by sending in her handmaid just as Leah had been used to deceive Jacob. Jacob did not know about Rachel switching places with her handmaid until the handmaid conceived.

50a. Reuben: Reuben would have been about 5 when he found the mandrakes. This would have been around late spring. The Testament of Reuben indicates that he cried when Rachel took them from her, although the verses says that Rachel asked Leah for them. Mandrakes were an herb that had the reputation of helping women get pregnant and therefore were valuable to Rachel. The Testament of Asher indicates that Asher and Issachar were both born close to the same time.

50b. Last sons: It says clearly that Leah believed that Jacob would exalt her for bearing him 6 sons. The last son was given to Rachel. Joseph was her only son and he was born in the last year of the 2nd 7 year period, or rather year 14 of the 21 years of labor for Laban. Calculating when the sons of Jacob does not lend much help in the way of establishing timelines and historical dates. The birth of Joseph is crucial to accurately pinpointing when Jacob entered Egypt and calculating back from there, when he started the years of labor with Laban.

50c. Last 7 years of labor: Jacob used some tricks of genetic inheritance to make his flocks more productive than Laban's flocks. HaShem blessed Jacob's flocks more than Laban's flocks.

51. Bereshit / Genesis 31: Jacob flees: Jacob was blessed and could not be cursed. However, Laban's sons turned his ear against them. It says that HaShem would not let Laban harm Jacob. Jacob recognized to his wives that it was HaShem who took Laban's flock and gave it to Jacob, not that Jacob stole the flock. It was HaShem who guided the males to mate with the speckled flocks. The reason Rachel stole Laban's idols, according to Rashi, was not to worship them, but to prevent Laban from using them for divination to locate Jacob and Jacob's family. Judah was about 10 and Joseph about 7 at this time.

Laban indicates that by Jacob leaving in secret, it was because Jacob had something to hide and Laban even accuses him of stealing Laban's idols. It is interesting that Jacob, in his wrath against Laban, tells us of the many troubles that he suffered during the 20 years. This should tell us that obedience to HaShem does not come without troubles. He suffered lack of sleep, blazing hot suns, cold nights, loss of some of his flock to wild animals, and loss of wages due to Laban's cheating. The pact between them was that HaShem should be judge over each of them while they were separate.

The pile of rocks represent earth which is a witness to all sins. The Hebrew stance is the same, they believe that the earth is witness to our sins. This is why the heavens and the earth will be destroyed at the end of the 7000 years, and at the final resurrection of the saints. This destruction will remove all witnesses to our past sins so that in *heaven* we are able to live free from all guilt. The heap of stones were called *Galeed, heap of witnesses*. This eventually became Galilee. It is imagined that this heap of rocks was a small heap of stones, but there is reason to believe that this heap of rocks was huge in stature, and could be seen from a distance.

51a. Dates: The year is 2265 A.T. or 1699 B.C. The Sedar Olam of the Jews places this date in 2205 A.M. The *Book of Jubilee* places this event in 2135 A.M. in the month of Nissan at the end of the Feast of Weeks (21ˢᵗ of the month). Abraham would have been 257 years old or 257 A.Ab. (Year of Abraham). This revised version agrees that these events took place in Nissan.

51b. Lydia and Isin: Eusebius supplies a list of late kings of Lydia but his list takes place during the kings of Israel, which is far too late for this period. Jerome (Je) supplies a more realistic list of dates (B.C.) for the kings of Lydia.

Lydia	Je	Lydia	Je
Cybele	1710	Iardanus	1276
Manes	1680	Timolus II	1250
Atys	1628	Omphale	1246
Lydus	1610	Agelaus	1221
Laud	1558	Caystrus	
Dionysus	1400	Ephesus	
Timolus	1380	Agron	1103
Tantalus	1360	Total	505 y

Gungunum defeats Isin and this ends the Isin Dynasty of the Babylonian Empire (II).

Menes is believed to have colonized the British Isles around the time he was conquering Crete and other Mediterranean locations. This includes Ireland as well. The peoples there became known as Druids or Celts and they are believed to have built Stonehenge around this time of Jacob.

52. Bereshit / Genesis 32: Esau approaches: Jacob's next concern was his brother Esau who he had not heard from in 20 years. The last he had heard, Esau was out to kill him. From Jacob's perspective, that had not changed. Jacob learned that Esau was coming to meet him with a force of 400 men. This number relates to the 400 years of Abraham's descendents being at odds in countries not their own. Jacob's prayer indicates his fear that his days might end, but he reminds HaShem of his promise.

52a. Jacob wrestles with the Angel: In the Masoretic version of the Bible, the term used for the man was *ish*, which means man, not angel, but Jacob refers to him as a divine being. The man must have been some kind of spiritual being as he renamed Jacob to Israel, *to prevail* + *el (God)*. Israel had succeeded in striving against divine beings and humans. The man must have been some divine being as this is the only time Jacob wrestled with such. Rashi, the Zohar, and Bereshit Rabbah all believe it was Lucifer that wrestled with Jacob.

53. Bereshit / Genesis 33: Esau and Jacob meet: The meeting turns out favorable to all appearances, although later, the two resume fighting. Jacob goes to Succoth, which means booths, dwelling, or huts. Jacob then arrived in Shechem. By this time Shem ben Noah has died. He purchased land which he called *El, God of Israel*. Since Jacob was called Israel by the divine being, this has a futuristic pun to it, Jacob's God and the God of the future Israel nation.

53a. Esau: Esau had married other Hittite women and one of his sons, Eliphaz, became the progenitor of the Amalekites which would be lifetime enemies of the Israelites. This same Eliphaz was a friend of Job. Esau still worshipped Isaac's God, so Eliphaz was a believer in HaShem as Job was.

54. Bereshit / Genesis 34-36: Dinah: According to the Testament of Levi, Levi was about 20 and according to this revised interpretation, this would make Dinah around 16. There are some Hebrew sources that believe she was younger, around 14. The Hittite father knew about the reputation of Jacob and feared a war with Jacob. If Jacob would agree to a contract between them it would alleviate the war. The sons decided to deceive the father and the town's men. Having them all circumcised at the same time would make every man of fighting age weak for a few days. Apparently, Jacob was unaware of the secret plan of his sons. Jacob didn't want war either. Levi and Simeon slew all the men of the town on the 3rd day while the other sons looted the city, including wives and children who became slaves of Jacob's forces. The selling of Joseph takes place shortly after this event as well, but is not covered in the Bible until Chapter 37.

Jacob was concerned about the other inhabitants of Canaan. If they all banded against him, Jacob would be outnumbered. Jacob takes his family to Bethel (later Bethlehem). HaShem then puts the fear of Jacob on all the people of the land so that none came against him.

54a. Israel: HaShem appears to Jacob and reaffirms that Jacob's name is now Israel as per the divine being's declaration on the night of the wrestling match. HaShem reveals to Jacob that HaShem's name is El Shaddai, *He who heals.* Jacob learns that the promise of Abraham will be fulfilled through Jacob's descendents. The site of HaShem's visit became known as Bethel for the first time, previous known as Luz.

54b. Benjamin: Rachel is blessed with a second son, Benjamin, but she dies in child birth. Isaac was still alive and Israel goes to see his father. Isaac died then at the age of 180 years old. Both Esau and Israel buried Isaac together. The date of the death of Isaac is 2288 A.T. Joseph is about 30 at the time of Isaac's death and was in Egypt at the time. Isaac died a mere 9 years before Jacob moved to Egypt.

54c. Esau / Edom: The land could not hold both Jacob's riches and Esau's. Esau takes his family and moves to Seir, or Edom. The Amalekites, eternal enemies of the Israelites, lived on the Eastern side of the Gulf of Aqaba (part of the Red Sea). During the times of the Judges, the Amalekites became a world class ruler, ruling over all Egypt (as a powerful dynasty), all Arabia, and parts of Greece. Their power extended up the borders of India. They ruled over Canaan during the time of the Judges, and the *Book of Judges* records a few of their invasions against the Israelites.

It is interesting that an entire chapter is devoted to the descendents of Esau, ben Isaac. His power was great in the land and at this time, there was peace between Edom and Israel (both Jacob and the people of Israel).

55. Bereshit / Genesis 37: Joseph: The Genesis narrative takes a step back in time in order to keep the story together and discusses the entire story of Joseph together apart from the other events. This same method is used in chapter 38, the story of Judah and Tamar. This was in a period of peace after the rape of Dinah, but very shortly after. Joseph's coat wasn't just one of many colors but was indicative of royalty. Like the coat of Yeshua (Jesus), the coat was without seams, sewn all as one (John 19:23).

Joseph had two dreams about his brothers bowing down to him. Two is a number of confirmation, meaning when HaShem does something like a dream TWICE it means that this dream is fated to come true, no matter what anyone does to try and stop it. It means that HaShem has determined that the events will happen no matter what. This was particularly insulting to the brothers as Joseph was the *youngest* (except for Benjamin) and thus was the last to rule by inheritance laws.

55a. Joseph Sold: He was sold for 20 pieces. The *Testament of Gad* reports that Joseph was actually sold for 30 pieces, but Gad kept 10 for himself secretly from his brothers. The Vugate (Latin) version of the Bible is the only one that reports 30 pieces. The *Book of Jubilee* reports that the news reached Israel about Joseph's death on Yom Kippur (10th of Tishrei) which falls in the Fall Season. This day is the day of repentance and yearly baptism in the Law of Moses. Bilhah is believed to have died just from the news of his death, but this can't be true as she was raped by Reuben after this time.

Joseph's tunic was dipped in blood and shown to Israel as proof that Joseph was killed by wild animals. Israel mourned over the death, but inside, he knew something was wrong. The tunic was not torn as they had reported as it should have been if a wild animal killed Joseph. He kept this belief to himself for 22 years.

Joseph is sold to Potifer and HaShem blesses Joseph's works. The *Testament of Judah* says that Potifer was the chief cook of the Pharaoh, but the Torah indicates that he was the Captain of the Guard and a Priest of On, (Genesis 41:50). Ginzberg says that the name of Potifer's wife was Zuleika and she was attracted to Joseph right away. Ginzberg indicates that Potifer's genitals were mutilated in an accident and thus he could not have sex with his wife. Through astrology, Zuleika learned that she was to have children through Joseph, which encouraged her to pursue him.

This later proved to be true as she did have children through Joseph when he married her daughter and they had children. The *Testament of Joseph* indicates that he was with Potifer 7 years before he was sent to prison under false evidence against him.

56. Bereshit / Genesis 38: Judah and Tamar: Once again, the story is separate from the actual chronological order in order to achieve a complete understanding of the events. Judah was around the age of 13-15 when he separated from his family. Given that Judah was born around 2255 A.T. by this revised version, that would mean that he married Shua's daughter, a Canaanite woman, around the year 2270 A.T. and had 3 sons by her; Er, Onan, and Shelah. When Er was around 13, Judah got him a wife by the name of Tamar, but Er died before Tamar could conceive by him. The rule of the time was that a widow usually married a younger brother of her late husband to give him an heir through the younger brother. Onan was less than a year younger than Er and became the next son to marry. Onan had a distaste to give his brother an heir and chose to masturbate (or possibly pull out before breeding Tamar during sex) and thus prevent her from having a son. HaShem punished Onan by killing him as well. Shelah was still too young, probably not yet in puberty, so Judah asked Tamar to wait. Shelah became of age around 2285 A.T., but Shua's daughter, Judah's wife, didn't want to take a chance on losing another son to Tamar, so she went behind Judah's back and got Shelah another wife from her own Canaanite clan. Due to her sin, the daughter of Shua, Judah's wife, died. After a period of mourning, Judah went up and saw a prostitute, who was Tamar in disguise. The verses say that Tamar was still wearing her widow's garb from Onan, so the timeline here is very tight. Tamar disguised herself as a whore. Judah didn't have the money, so he left a few articles for a promise to pay her. When Judah went back to pay her, he couldn't find the harlot. This would have been about the year 2286 A.T. Judah heard that Tamar was with child about 3 months later and he was angry that she had whored herself. Judah was about to have her burned when she showed him the articles that he had left and Judah realized his sin against Tamar. Judah was about 31 years old at the time of this confrontation. She gave birth to twins, Perez and Zerah. The twins were about the age of 12 when they entered Egypt with Jacob in 2298 A.T. The story barely fits within the time allotted, but it does fit when given the young ages of marriage for all the males involved. David was a descendant of Perez, and therefore a descendant of Judah.

57. Bereshit / Genesis 39: Back to Joseph in Egypt: Potifer quickly recognized that Joseph's God was blessing Joseph in all that he did and made Joseph the head of his house so that he could profit from Joseph's success. Potifer's wife approached Joseph to seduce him every day, but Joseph refused. In her anger, she frames him for rape and has him thrown into prison. This didn't stop HaShem from blessing Joseph and Joseph quickly rose in the ranks of the prisoners to the top prisoner in charge. Here we see that HaShem's blessings do not prevent things from happening that appear to be bad, but continues to bless the obedient. It was through this prison experience that Joseph was later able to save his family from famine. If the testaments are correct, Joseph was about 24 when he was thrown into prison. Joseph was born in 2258 A.T. Teti I was the Pharaoh at this time.

In Egypt, Teti has inscriptions where he cast out all Asiatics from Egypt at this time through war. This did not include the Hebrew slaves. To the south, the Nubians were rebelling as well and they too were defeated by Amenemhet (Teti). Amenemhet ruled over Ethiopia for a time as his name is listed in the Ethiopian list as Amen Emhat I (Amenemhat). We can see here how modern historians created two people out of one simply because of a miss-spelling. A Stela of Nessumont mentions Sesostris association with his father, Amenemhat after the start of the famine. David Down and John Ashton prefer to match Joseph to Sesostris, given that the vizier of Sesostris was a powerful man, but they seem to ignore the famine factor which took place during the time of Amenemhet.

58. Bereshit / Genesis 40: The Dreams: A short time after being put in prison, Joseph interprets the dreams of the baker and the cupbearer. He makes a statement that HaShem is the interpreter of dreams. This same statement was made by Daniel to Nebuchadnezzar. It is true humility to give HaShem the credit for all success. Taking credit for your own skills and/or genius can only come from a prideful heart. The interpretations came true three days later on the Pharaoh's birthday celebration. This was 2 years before the Pharaoh's dreams about the famine.

59. Bereshit / Genesis 41: Pharaoh's Dreams: Once again, Joseph does not dare take the credit for interpreting dreams, but gives the credit to HaShem. Joseph indicates that the fact that Pharaoh had the same dream twice means that it was determined by HaShem to happen, no matter what or who tried to stop it. Joseph is made the 2nd most powerful man in Egypt. It is believed in this revised version that Joseph was actually the leader of a minor dynasty that paralleled the 6th/12th dynasty which is the 11th dynasty. Joseph was then married to the daughter of Potifer and during the next 7 years of plenty, they had 2 sons. Joseph's name was changed to an Egyptian name, Zaphenath-Paneah or Ipi-ankhu (sometimes pronounced Pi-ankah). There is evidence that the Egypt was already going through a food surplus period of time (10 years according to David Rohl) but that the dreams suggested 7 more years of plenty. David Rohl says the years of plenty started in the 3rd year of Amenemhet. There is a storehouse that is recorded, *Storehouse of Ankhu (ankah or Joseph's other name).*

David Rohl shows the record Nile markings during the years of plenty bear out the story, these markings taking place during the rule of Amenemhet. Dr. Breasted mentions an inscription by Sesostris in Wadi Halfa about a *General Mentuhotep*, which was the name of the 11th dynasty pharaoh. It is suggested here that dynasty 11 was not truly an independent dynasty at all, but under the leadership of Joseph (Mentuhotep) was a sub-dynasty of dynasty 12.

The Canal of Joseph was the main answer to the years of famine. By channeling some of the Nile into a separate canal during the years of high waters, these same waters could avert the dry periods of the Nile so that the drought years were not as severe. This canal was cut into the Faiyum region of Egypt. Herodotus calls this the Bahr Yussef (Canal of Joseph). Lake Moeris was created from this and had not previously existed prior to this time. Moeris is the Greek name for Amenemhet's normal name of Nimuriaria.

59a. Famine: The 7 years of famine started when Joseph was 38 years old. Joseph had just turned 30 at the end of the year of the dreams of the pharaoh and 31 during the 1st year of plenty predicted by the dreams. This is believed to be another type of Yeshua who started His ministry at the age of 31. The years of plenty would be evenly matched the years of Yeshua Messiah's years of ministry before He was *cut off*. Amenemhet was in his 20th year of rule when the years of famine started.

This was another world wide famine (Genesis 41:56 and the Midrash Rabbah, reaching as far as China. It most definitely reached Canaan where Jacob's family was affected by the famine. In China, the Shang dynasty beings with a new ruler who records a 7 year famine during his entire rule. This famine caused Egypt to become allies with Athens (still called Attica) when Egypt supplied them with food.

Inscriptions at Sarbut el-Khadem refer to Joseph by yet another name, Ptahwer who was the son of Yata (Yatu or Jacob). It was common for the Egyptians to have up to 7 names, which has led to some errors in modern historians by causing them to create several people for the same person, because they didn't know that the different names referred to the same person.

The revised date for the start of the famine is 2297 A.T. or 1667 B.C. The Hebrew chronology gives it a date of 2237 A.M. Joseph was 38 years old and Abraham would have been 289 years old. *The Book of Jasher* gives this event the year of 2299 A.M.

59b. China: The Shang Dynasty is tied with Egyptian history through this famine of 7 years. There have been only 2 recorded famines of this length since Noah at this time. The first was the famine of Abraham. The famine of China could not refer to the famine of Abraham as the conventional dates closely match that of Joseph's famine. The Shang Dynasty is considered to be the first *true* dynasty in China. The Xia Dynasty had just ended and was considered a myth for many years. The Shang Dynasty got its name from Shang Ti, the supreme god over the lesser god of China. Ancestor worship derived from this religion. It was toward the end of this dynasty that China began to colonize Japan.

Shang Dynasty	Yrs	Revised A.T. / B.C.	Family changed to Chang		Revised A.T. / B.C.
Ch'en Tang	13	2297 / 1667	Hsiao Hsin	21	2663 / 1301
T'ai Chia	33	2309 / 1655	Hsiao Yi	28	2683 / 1281
Wu Ting	29	2341 / 1623	Wu Ting	59	2700 / 1264
T'ai Keng	25	2369 / 1595	Tsu Keng	7	2758 / 1206
Hsiao Chia	17	2383 / 1571	Tsu Chia	33	2764 / 1200
Yung Chi	12	2399 / 1555	Lin Hsin	6	2796 / 1168
T'ai Mou	75	2410 / 1544	Keng Ting	21	2801 / 1163
Chung Ting	13	2484 / 1480	Wu Yi	4	2821 / 1143
Wai Jen	15	2496 / 1468	T'ai Ting	3	2824 / 1140
Ho Tan Chia	9	2510 / 1454	Ti Yi	37	2826 / 1138
Tsu Yi	19	2518 / 1446	Ti Hsin-Chou	32	2862 / 1102
Tsu Hsin	16	2536 / 1428	Ven Vang	19	2894 / 1070
Wu Chia	25	2551 / 1413	**New Dynasty of Vu Veng**		
Tsu Ting	32	2575 / 1389	Vu Veng		2913 / 1051
Nan Keng	25	2606 / 1358			
Yang Chia	7	2630 / 1334			
P'an Keng	28	2636 / 1328			

To the west in Xin Xiang between Kazakhstan and Mongolia, mummies have been found that were perfectly preserved. These mummies were pure Caucasian and pure Oriental, side by side. The caucasion mummies were so well preserved that they still had skin and hair on them. The fabrics on the mummies were also well preserved and were the fabrics made in early Central and Eastern Europe (Greece). At this time, the mummies give evidence that Caucasian and Oriental lived peacefully side by side. The size of the mummies show that the men and women were not any different than the average height of our modern man and woman. These mummies pre-date the Shang Dynasty by only a few years or during the time of the famine.

The Shang Dynasty ended when Vu Vang defeated Chou (the last Shang ruler) and brought in the Chou Dynasty. The last ruler of the Shang Dynasty was cruel and the queen was worse. She instituted torture devices that been known to be the worst known to man. They instituted perverse sexual practices. She was the one that instituted the practice of the binding of oriental feet due to the fact that her own feet were so small. When a king died, it had become the practice to bury hundreds of slaves and prisoners with the king, some alive but mostly sacrificed.

60. Bereshit / Genesis 42-47: Jacob moves to Egypt: Joseph decides to test his brothers. Joseph sets them up by putting their money back in their food bags to take home. This takes place in the first year of the famine. Simeon was left behind for ransom as it was Simeon who was behind Joseph's capture. During the second year, 2298 A.T., Jacob calls HaShem by El Shaddai, the name that HaShem gave to him many years earlier. The sons were astonished on the second trip when Joseph invited them to his table and he had them seated in correct order, without conferring with them. Joseph then sets up Benjamin with a stolen object. The other sons plead with Joseph still not knowing who he is until Joseph can't take it any longer and reveals himself.

60a. HaShem's Plan: Joseph holds no hate or anger toward his brothers as he reveals that he understands that all that happened to him was to send him ahead of his brothers to save them from the famine. *It was not them that sent him to Egypt, but HaShem!*

60b. Jacob in Egypt: Jacob has another visit in a dream from HaShem assuring him to go to Egypt. Jacob never fails to check with HaShem first. This is the first rule of obedience to HaShem whether a Jew from 4500 years ago or yesterday. Jacob is 130 years old. He lives his last 17 years in Egypt. It is coincidental that Joseph's first 17 years of life was in Jacob's care and Jacob's last 17 years of life was in Joseph's care. In the list of people that went down, Perez's sons were listed. This causes some concern about the Judah/Tamar timeline. Perez was very young when he had these two sons. A total of 70 of Jacob's family was in Egypt. The Septuagint indicates that there were 75 people that went down to Egypt. The Hebrew chronology indicates that Jochebed (mother of Moses) was born the same year as the entry into Egypt.

The reason that the Pharaoh left them in Goshen (a northern region of Egypt) was due to the fact that they were shepherds, an occupation abhorrent to Egyptians and the Pharaoh didn't want any conflict with his own people. On the tomb of a nobleman of Egypt, in the 12th dynasty, there is a pictograph of Asiatics entering Egypt peacefully into the city of Avaris, which is in Goshen. Long haired sheep were known in this area which is the kind of sheep related to ancient Israel and unknown to Egypt. David Down offers a papyrus by a 12th dynasty woman who insists that it her right to own slaves, but there is no evidence that this refers to the Israelites. Egypt had slaves before Jacob arrived there.

In the city of Avaris, pits filled with dead bones of slaves that were persecuted later in this same dynasty, were found. Most of them were Hebrew, but there were other slaves as well. The city of Avaris lasted until its downfall when the Amalekites took their last stand there and were defeated by Samuel and Saul.

60c. Dates: The date of the actual move to Egypt is 2298 A.T. or 1666 B.C. The Hebrew date is 2238 A.M. The *Book of Jubilees* gives 2172 A.M. The *Book of Jasher* gives 2300 A.M. The *Testament of Judah* gives 2295 A.M. The *Testament of Levi* gives 2287 A.M. James Ussher (King James Bible), Floyd Nolan Jones, and Frank Klassen all agree on 2298 A.M. David Down and John Ashton agree on 1677 B.C. This would be Abraham's 290th year. Joseph is 39 and Jacob is 130.

61. Bereshit / Genesis 48: Death of Israel: Amram ben Kohath is born the year before Israel dies. By this reckoning, he was younger than his future wife and aunt, Jochebed. On his death bed, Israel blesses Joseph's sons, the younger first which is a switch from tradition where usually the older son gets the best blessing. Jacob too was the younger and managed to get the blessing from Esau. The Hebrew Chronology indicates that Esau tried to stop the burial of Jacob, but failed. This same record says that Jacob/Israel was buried on Tishrei 15th (Feast of Tabernacles and the Birth of Yeshua Messiah). The Hebrew chronology verifies that Amram was born just before the death of Israel. The *Testament of Amram* is one of the Dead Sea Scrolls and one of the few testaments that has remain uncorrupted.

The last words of Israel were predictions of what would befall his sons and their descendents. Judah is declared to be the leader of them in the future (and from his line, the kings would come). Zebulun would be the ship builder of the nation in the future. Israel was buried in the cave purchased by Abraham for Sarah. The embalming process took 40 days. His brothers were worried that now that Israel was dead, Joseph would seek revenge against what they did to him, but Joseph remains steadfast in assuring them that while they meant him harm, HaShem, Shaddai meant what they did to Joseph for good.

61a. Dates: The death of Israel takes place in 2315 A.T., 1649 B.C., and 2255 A.M. by Hebrew Chronology. Israel was 147 years old.

61b. India: This appears to be about the time of the beginning of the Magadha or Bahadratha Dynasty of India (from Puranas). India won a battle against Assyria around this time.

61c. Teti/Amenemhet assassinated: The *Story of Sinuhe* is about the assassination of Amenemhet. This story is often attributed to Moses and his escape from Egypt around his 40th year, but this revised version rejects that as Joseph is still alive and places Moses much later. Sesostris / Pepi rules after his father. He grows to fear the growing numbers of the Hebrews, but he obviously fears the power of Joseph more. While Joseph is alive, he shows favor to the Hebrew still.

61d. Hammurabi of Babylon II: The code of Hammurabi has been attributed to him, but was more likely written by his father. The code was known by Hammurabi's predecessors. Hammurabi conquered Larsa and Isin around his 16th year. He then went on to conquer the Assyrians. By the end of his rule, he ruled most of the Mesopotamian area, giving viability to this new Babylonian Empire (II). To the west, the Kassites (Hittites of Abraham) have started to grow in power. They would eventually bring an end to the second Babylonian Empire.

Gandash starts to rule the Kassites around the time of Hammurabi's son. Agum II is said to have defeated Samsuditana of Babylon and ended the Babylonian Empire. Samsuiluna, son of Hammurabi, managed to hold Babylon together for a while and destroys Uruk and Ur, burning them both to the ground. He managed to win a few battles against the Kassites, but eventually, Agum defeated him. The history of Babylon becomes blurred from this point on. George Roux believes that it was the Hittites who destroyed Babylon. It is possible that the Hittites and the Kassites are the same people, but not assured. The Kassites are the first known historians to keep track of events by the year of the king other than Biblical records.

61f. Sparta: Eusebius traces back the Spartan history, but it's sketchy. He gets his information from Diodorus. Castor was the first to write about the history of Sparta, but his works have been lost. The following list of rulers from Eusebius is to be taken with a grain of salt. The list of these kings have been traced back from a more secure dating for Sparta of 1101 (a related date to the destruction of Troy). The date, 1101 B.C., is the beginning of the Heraclidae Dynasty of Sparta.

Sparta	B.C.	Sparta	Reference	B.C.
Spartus	1609	Cynortas		1320
Myceneus	1584	Oebalius		1268
Myles	1508	Tyndareus		1239
Eurotas	1460	Menelaus	Trojan War 1181	1211
Lacedaemon	1417	Orestes		1171
Amyclas	1380	Tsiamneus		1156
Aigalus	1330			

62. Bereshit / Genesis 50:22-26: Death of Joseph: *The Book of Jasher* indicates that the Pharaoh's adviser, Zapnah, told the Pharaoh that the people of Jacob would join with the enemies of Egypt. Sesostris had the bones of Joseph closely guarded and Joseph was not allowed a proper Hebrew burial. It would be Moses who secures the bones and buries Joseph in Israel. According to this same record in Jasher, the enslavement started in 2377 A.T. 8 years after the death of Joseph. The remaining patriarchs die in the next 20 years after Joseph's death. Benjamin and Levi are the last to die. Hosea 13:1 says that Ephraim Ben Joseph incurred some kind of guilt through a false god, Baal and it caused his death shortly after Joseph's.

62a. Date of Joseph's Death: This revised version gives him a date of 2369 A.T. or 1595 B.C. The Hebrew Chronology dates his death in 2309 A.M. Joseph was 110 years old and Abraham would have been 361 years old. The estimated deaths of the other patriarchs are not given in the Bible, but through their testaments are as follows. Joseph died in the 42nd year of Pepi / Sesostris, pharaoh of Egypt. Sesostris ruled for another 50 years after Joseph died and is the pharaoh responsible for the subjection of the Jews before Moses was born. Moses was born 14 years after the death of Sesostris.

Patriarchs	Death Year A.T.	Death Age	Patriarchs	Death Year A.T.	Death Age
Zebulun	2372	114	Dan	2380	125
Simeon	2373	120	Gad	2383	127
Reuben	2377	125	Naphtali	2388	132
Asher	2377	120	Benjamin	2390	120
Issachar	2379	122	Levi	2391	137
			Subjection of Egypt after Levi died.		

62b. Genealogy of Joseph to Joshua: Joshua was from the line of Joseph through Ephraim.

Patriarch	David Rohl B.C.	Revised	Patriarch	David Rohl B.C.	Revised
Joseph	1667	2290/1674	Tahan	1547	
Ephraim	1647		Laadan	1527	
Beriah	1627		Ammihud	1507	
Rephah	1607		Elishama	1487	
Resheph	1587		Nun	1467	
Telah	1567		Joshua	1447	2513/1451

62c. Patriarchs of Israel: Hebrew chronology = Seder Olam, S.T. = Samaritan Text; D/A = David Down / John Asher

Name	Hebrew	Jubilee	LXX	S.T.	Ussher	D/A	Revised A.T. / B.C. / Yr Rule		
Abraham	1948	1876	3334	2249	2008	1950	2008	1956	2083
Ishmael (false)	2035	1967			2095	1863	2095	1869	2171
Isaac	2048	1980	3434	2349	2108	1850	2108	1856	2184
Jacob	2108	2046	3494	2409	2168	1790	2168	1796	2289
Joseph	2199	2134	3585	2500	2258	1699	2258	1706	2316
Elders									2370
Moses	2368	2330			2433	1525	2432	1532	2473

CHAPTER 8

SUMMARY OF GENESIS

63. Summary: The Book of Bereshit (Hebrew name) / Genesis covers the history of the world for the first 2400 years. As mentioned, this revised version believes that HaShem did not write in *mysteries*, but is a God of *full disclosure* of His plan for mankind. There are many types and archetypes in Genesis that this revised version did not delve into for fear of becoming too fanatical about such types, which can be harmful in reverse ways. Still the predictions of Yeshua Messiah (Jesus the Christ) through the types and many of the details about the coming Messiah's life through these types are significant and could not be avoided.

The history of the Genesis world is accurate and HaShem left no detail out which would help us to understand the chronology, important to the understanding of HaShem's plan for the world. The following diagram is close to proper scale of the event timelines for Genesis. Shown in this diagram are books that are not included in the Bible, but considered of some Hebrew authority, barring the Epic of Gilgamesh which is totally Assyrian / Sumerian literature.

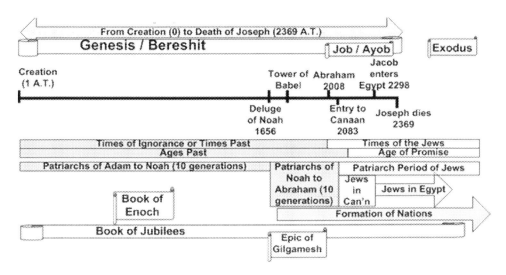

The Hebrew name for the book of Genesis is *Be_re_sheeth, or "in the beginning"*. The plan of HaShem is accurate but it could only be discerned with an accurate history of the world. For a more complete version of the history, should anyone be interested, please refer to the *Revised History of the Ancient World*, by this author. It is 700 pages of the most boring history you could ever want to read but I believe that it is one of the most accurate histories ever written.

CHAPTER 9

Yovel through the Bible

64. Ruth and the Yovel: The story of Ruth is about the ancestor of David but it gives us some clues as to the Yovel. The Yovel count started when Adam and Eve took possession of the land, after their exile from Eden. But there is a second Yovel, the "Israel Only Yovel". The Israel Yovel count started after the death of Joshua, in Judges when the last of the tribes finally took possession of the land of Israel.

Jephthah began his first year in a Yovel year, the 300ᵗʰ year of the occupation of Israel. The events of Ruth took place at this time. Boaz was a kinsman that was able to redeem the land for Naomi. The shoe was the proof and Boaz was able to redeem the land for Naomi, but this had to take place in a Yovel year, according to the rules of the Jubilee. Soon after this, Boaz became a judge in the land of Israel, but he was known by the Hebrew name of Ibzan. His name in the Septuagint is Abaissan. Boaz is another derivative of those two names.

65. Hezekiah: Later, during the time of the kings, Hezekiah has been ruling and then he gets a message from Isaiah, the prophet that he is to get his affairs in order he was going to die. Hezekiah makes a major act of repentance and Isaiah is ordered to turn around and go back to Hezekiah. Hezekiah is given another 15 years to live. Along with this, Isaiah gives Hezekiah a sign. The land of Israel is going to be able to live that year on the crops of the year before AND the next year as well. So this is two

SABBATH years in a row, which only happens every 50 years; year 49 and year 50 of the Yovel, of which, year 50 is the Yovel year.

Hezekiah and Sennacherib and Earth changes course:

A.T.	3246		3247		3248		3249		3250		3251		3252		Rev.
Yovel	Yr 46		Yr 47		Yr 48		Yr 49 - Shabbat		Yovel Year		Yr 1		Yr 2		
B.C.	718		717		716		715		714		713		712		Greg.
A.M.	3210		3211		3212		3213		3214		3215		3216	3217	Heb
Seasons	Sp	Su	Au	W	Sp	Su	Au	W	Sp	Su	Au	W	Sp	Su	Au	W

Isaiah ben Amos the prophet

Hezek.	Yr 11	Yr 12	Yr 13	Yr 14	Yr 15	Yr 16	Yr 17
Sargon / Sennacherib	Attack on Judah against Hezekiah / Attack on Lachish against Taharqa		X X	Sargon / Sennacherib retreats back to Nineveh for good.			
	Yr 6	Yr 7	Yr 8	Yr 9	Yr 10	Yr 11	Yr 12
	Fall of Ashdod						
Taharqa	Yr 4	Yr 5	Yr 6	Yr 7	Yr 8	Yr 9	Yr 10
Sethos	Yr 11	Yr 12	Yr 13	Yr 14	Yr 15	Yr 16	Yr 17
Harmais	Yr 4	Yr 5	Yr 6	Yr 7	Yr 8	Usurper of Sethos dynasty	
Takelot II	Yr 14	Yr 15	Yr 16	Yr 17	Yr 18	Yr 19	Yr 20
Shoshq III	Yr 12	Yr 13	Yr 14	Yr 15	Yr 16	Yr 17	Yr 18

Earth changes its course to 365.2422 days per year in 15th year of Shoshenq III and 14th year of Hezekiah

Isaiah tells Hezekiah to ask for a sign. Hezekiah says that it is nothing for HaShem to ask to move the sun forward, so he asks for HaShem to move the sun backward 10 Degrees. Anyone with an elementary knowledge of the solar system would understand that the sun is not the object that moved, but rather, the earth was moved in its orbit. This caused the shift of the earth's orbit to change from 360 days per year to 364.2422 days per year. This event took place in the year 3249 A.T. or 3249 from the year of Creation. According to the "Revised Chronology of the Bible", this year is equivalent the year 715 B.C.

Shortly after this year, every calendar of every known civilization of the time had to correct their calendars for the change in the yearly day count. The Papyrus Leiden, Egyptian document, records that the moon changed its course from 30 days a month to 29-30 days a month. The Bamboo Books of China also record that in the 10th year of emperor Kwai of the Yu Dynasty the skies changed their course. Egypt had to add 5 "Epogomenal Days to their year. These 5 days became a short 13th month in their calendar. This calendar was later adopted by Julius Caesar to create the Julian calendar of 365 days per year. This was corrected later by Augustus Caesar when 5 extra days proved to be too many adjustment days. India and China adopted a multiple calendar system, one lunar and one solar. The Greeks went through a few iterations finally resulting in a Metonic Calendar of varying number of days per year.

66. Yeshua Messiah (Jesus the Christ): While there is no further direct reference (or even indirect) of the Yovel, Yeshua Messiah was crucified in the year 4000 A.T. or exactly to the day after Adam and Even were cast out of Eden. This is equivalent to Nissan 14, 4000 A.T. or 37 A.D.

This is a Yovel year, the 80th Yovel. This part has to be calculated based on an accurate recreation of history from the Bible "Revised Chronology of the Bible". Since Yeshua Messiah is very key to understanding the Yovel (and vice versa), tying him to the Yovel in the year of His crucifixion is of a great deal of understanding to the overall Plan of HaShem.

CHAPTER 10

GENESIS REVELATION CONNECTION

67. Genesis Connection: While Genesis was HaShem's way of showing us His plan and His work over the next 7000 years, Revelation is the culmination of that work, showing us the *End of Days*. Genesis has many types and shadows *of things to come*. To list some of those here:

The predicted event or time	Approximate Genesis references
The overall plan of Hashem for 7000 years of history	Genesis 1 / 2 Week of Creation
The coming of the Messiah to defeat Satan	Genesis 3 Punishment of Adam and Eve
The coming of the Messiah	Ark of Noah as a Type
History of the world	Noah's life before the flood as type
Details about the coming Messiah	Isaac (see chapter on Isaac types)
People resulting after the Crucifixion	Esau and Jacob
More details about Messiah	Joseph

From the end of the Book of Genesis to the book of Daniel, the entire history of the world is covered up to the Crucifixion of Yeshua Messiah. History can be traced chronologically through the Old Testament books and even into the New Testament books up to around 70 A.D. This chart is an overall look at 7000 years. The blocks above show the heavenly location of different peoples. The upper white areas are heaven. The gray area is the worldly location of the different peoples. Satan is shown as the darker gray in Perdition. For 1993 years, Israel was the focus of HaShem. After the crucifixion of Yeshua, the Bride is the focus of HaShem for another 1993 years. During the Millennium, Yeshua will rule on earth as King along with the martyred saints. Many believe that the believers resurrected will rule with Christ on earth. The far left of this chart is Genesis 1 and the far right is Revelation 22:6.

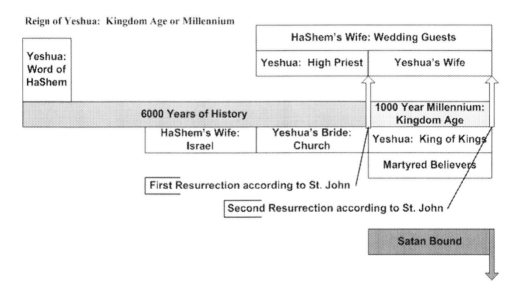

68. Revelations 1: Prediction of the Coming of Jesus: When Jesus arrives the second time, it will be with the clouds and *every eye shall see him.* This includes believers and non-believers. Everyone will know that He has come. The entire earth shall wail Him. It even implies that those who impaled Him will see Him, so that not only the living will see Him, but the dead as well.

68a. John sees the *Son of man*: He sees Him in the midst of 7 candlesticks. The Son of man declares specifically that *He lived, died, and is alive!* The candlesticks are the 7 churches that existed in Asia at the time of John's writing. The stars were the angels of those churches.

The symbolism is heavy here, but we have no need to worry about proper interpretation as He gives us the interpretation.

69. Revelations 2-3: Seven Churches: Each of the churches received a different message. It is unknown if these churches are symbolic of churches throughout the 1930 years of the Age of Grace or if they are the church of that time. Attempts have been made to determine each church (in chronological order) for a given time period (for example, each one representing about 280 years of history A.D.). Unfortunately, without a proper and truthful history of 70 A.D. to 2000 A.D. it is impossible to make proper time period breakouts for each church. Sadly, this author admits that history has been convoluted over time and corrupted. Looking at modern events in the U.S., one can see that certain factions are determined to re-write history to their own agenda. And it could be that all 7 churches existed throughout the 2000 years. It is very likely that each church does represent a period of time in chronological order of the existence of the church. The first one mentions the Nicolaitans which was early in Christian history. It is *conjecture* at this point.

69a. Ephesus: Ephesus was complimented on searching out false apostles and leaders. Since this work of John was written at the beginning of Christian history, it seems that the warnings are against the church that it was possible for them to lose their star as a valid church if they did not heed the warnings against him. The one promise to those who overcome is that we will eat of the *Tree of Life* that was refused to Adam and Eve. This is a strong tie back to Genesis directly, showing that what happened in Genesis was directly connected to Revelations.

69b. Smyrna: The interesting thing here is that John refers to the Christians as Jews and others who claim to be Jews but are not. The term Christian didn't come about until much later, but was a sub-division of the Jewish community. There were Pharisees, Sadducees, and then the *believers of Jesus*. It is the view point here that were never intended to be Christian and Jew, but one people of God. The tribulation of 10 days is a mystery here. It should be obvious that tribulations and tortures for many were not exactly 10 days. This must be symbolic to some reality that had yet to take place at the time of Revelation's writing. Those who persevere will get the *Crown of Life* and shall not suffer the experience of the second death.

69c. Pergamos: This mentions the name of Balaam, a prophet of God for the unbelievers. Balaam was able to prophecy the words of HaShem, but he was not a prophet of the Jews. He was known as a prophet of HaShem, but to the Gentiles. When he tried to prophecy against the Jews (in particular Jacob), HaShem changed his prophecy to be for them, three times. He was unable to go against God's blessing on the Jews to curse them. This was the accusation against this church that they took up the cult of Balaam. However, it points out that Balaam did teach Balak how to defeat the Israelites by tempting them into sin. This warning was for the churches who invite prophets in who teach against the Word of HaShem. The promise is that we will each receive a new name if we overcome.

69d. Thyatira: This church received a warning against Jezebel, the wife of Ahab. Jezebel was her own cult and tried to destroy the prophets of HaShem. She taught the worship of idols and false gods. She is the chief example of the whore of Babylon. The reward here is that he/she who overcomes will rule over nations. This particular promise leads us to believe that this Church is only for particular people. Not everyone can rule over the nations or there would be no one to lead.

69e. Sardis: This church does not seem to be faring too well and had a reputation of being dead, instead of living. They are not given any compliments but warned to keep watch for He who comes as a thief in the night, Jesus.

69f. Philadelphia: This seems to be a powerful church. The servants of Satan will be made to bow at their feet. They are to be kept from the hour of temptation which will come upon the world. Those who overcome will live in the Temple of HaShem and will never leave. They will know the new name of HaShem, which has not yet been revealed.

69g. Laodiceans: This church is neither hot nor cold, but luke warm and as such, not fit. This church does indeed seem to represent the state of the modern churches which profess to be rich and do not need HaShem. Being a wealthy large church seems to be the focus of the modern churches and as such, they claim to be blessed by HaShem for their wealth. The message of these churches has been watered down to entertain the masses and bring in more people to give more money to make them even richer. Clarence Larkin wrote that the majority of churches have given in to having become social clubs providing entertainment rather than speaking the *mind of HaShem.* He wrote this in 1928.

This church more than the others, gives us a reason to believe that the 7 churches are a progression through the 2000 years of Church history showing how each period of time has specific strengths and weaknesses within the true church. This work excludes physical churches from being included in the true church, but rather, the true church is comprised of individuals around the world hidden within the worldly church.

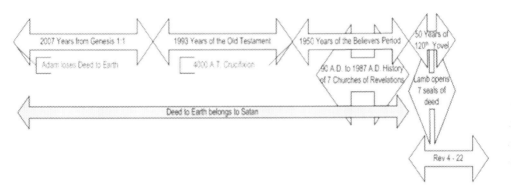

70. Revelations 4: John is brought before the Throne of HaShem. The meanings of the beasts is subjective in interpretation, unless it is told to us. To presume that we understand HaShem's words and symbolism without being told is pure ego and pride. The sea of glass is the sea of martyrs and at this point of the vision, it is empty.

71. Revelations 5: The Scroll: This scroll or book is the *Deed to the heavens, the earth, and to all within.* This is the deed that Adam lost to Satan when he sinned. It is sealed with 7 seals. Never mind that it is in the hands of the Almighty, it is still a deed to the claim on earth. This is the single most important connection to Genesis that we have. This deed can only be retrieved or unsealed by the innocent Lamb of God, our *kinsman.* John was upset that no one seemed worthy, but he was told that there was one worthy, the descendent of David, the slain lamb with 7 horns.

The common interpretation of the 7 seals is that they are all opened within a 7 year period, referred to as the Tribulation or week of Jacob's Trouble. This concept ignores the Yovel contract that is attached to the

Deed or the Scroll. It is the belief here that the 7 seals are opened over 1 Yovel period, with each seal and the consequences of that seal taking place over 7 years. This starts 50 years before the end of the 6000 years of HaShem's working week, 5951 A.T. (which translates to 1988 A.D. in this revised history version). This 50 year period is *the End of Days or End of Wrath.*

72. Revelations 6: Opening the Seals: Each of the seals brings on some form of HaShem's wrath. The consequences of each seal takes 7 years to accomplish. The seals are opened *in heaven, not on earth.* They are opened by Yeshua the Messiah. This means that at the opening of the seals, Yeshua has not come back for His second coming, He is still in heave with the Father. He remains in heaven until the opening of the 7th seal, and all the trumpets and vials. This contradicts those who believe that Jesus will come back before the earth suffers the consequences of the 7 seals (commonly believed to be pre-tribulation resurrection).

72a. First Seal: Thunder initiates this seal, followed by a white horse. He that sat on him had a bow. This rider went forth riding and conquering. This does not describe Yeshua, just because it has a white horse and Yeshua is still in heaven, not conquering. This seal takes place between the years of 1988 – 1994 A.D. Clarence Larkin proposes that this rider is the Anti-Christ who has not yet come into power. He has a bow, but no arrow. This author believes that this is the rise of the nations against HaShem who have not yet achieved full power.

72b. Second Seal: The horse was red, symbolic of blood. The rider was given power to take peace from earth so that men would begin the terrible violence against one another that was seen at the end of the days before the Flood of Noah. Since 1967, in America, crime has steadily increased, including violent crimes of murder, rape, and sex trafficking. In 1983, the rise of the Muslim religion (responsible for so much violence) began to rise through the creation of the PLO. It is the belief here that this rider is the Spirit of the Anti-Christ, filling men with lusts and desires and violence. The consequences of this seal take place during the years of 1995 – 2001 A.D.

72c. Third Seal: The horse was black and the rider had scales to measure. This refers to the balance of food in the world. An article in

U.S. News Today in March 2008, tells us that grains used for food were being used for fuel instead. This has created a huge food shortage. Food prices over the last few years have doubled and tripled. This same report indicated that the price of food for a day in certain countries was equal to a day's pay. It is this year, 2008 A.D. that the economic crisis hits the entire world. The dates of this seal take place during 2002 – 2008 A.D.

72d. Fourth Seal: This is the last horse and the horse was pale, with Death as its rider. He was given power to destroy with hunger and disease. During this time, hunger and starvation are evident in the millions. Over the course of the years, 2009-2015 A.D., the number of those starving to death will equal one fourth of the overall population. This seal and the 3rd seal have already taken place, giving evidence that the *resurrection* has not yet taken place as many Christians believed it would. Those churches still preaching *revival* are not preaching from the Spirit of HaShem. From now on, there will be no more revivals but a great falling away. Christians are seeking churches that *entertain* and give them good news, but there is only one bit of good news, and that is that Yeshua Messiah is the Savior.

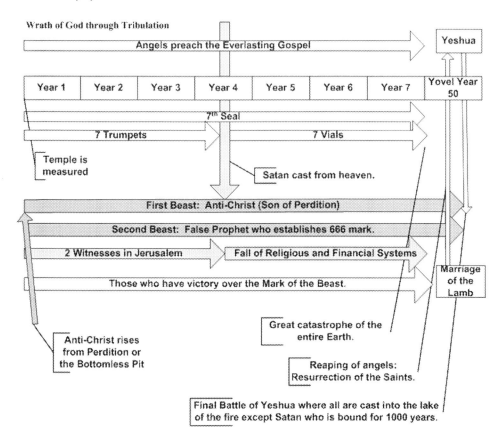

72e. Fifth Seal: The martyrs of HaShem are asking Him how much longer and He replies that they must wait for a *little season*. In Revelation, a week is referred to as 7 years, so a little season would be a little longer than that, perhaps 3 weeks. The souls are still under the altar and not yet in the Sea of Glass. HaShem says to them that they must wait until their fellow brethren would be killed for His Name, as they had been. This means that there are true believers still on earth and have not yet been resurrected. The dates of this seal take place between 2016 and 2022 A.D.

During this time, the tide of the belief turns and liberals and atheists have labeled Christianity as a religion of hate and some groups have been classified as *terrorists*. This legalizes the unbelievers to kill Christians without any boundaries. The rise of Islam who also see Christians as pagans who deserve to be killed takes place during this time.

Nebuchadnezzar had a dream around 600 B.C. and Daniel was the young prophet that HaShem chose to interpret the dream. Skipping to the base of the image, where the feet and toes of the image is made of iron and clay. Iron and clay do not mix well. Hydrogen and oxygen chemically combine to make water, changing the characteristics of both hydrogen and oxygen. Iron and clay cling to one another but yet remain two separate entities, never fully combining. It is obvious that the iron represents the ruling Roman Empire (Christian or not), but this author believes that this representation does not represent the *true Christian, but rather the worldly ruler ship of Christianity*. The clay represents the rise of the Muslim religion and once again, not the good Muslim, but the rise of the totalitarian Muslim who believes that anyone who is not Muslim must die or become slaves. The fact that both are together, means that the Muslim religion is going to quickly rise to power and be in conflict with the ruling Roman Empire but yet they will both be in power together. This prediction has come true amazingly fast as the Muslims have invaded Europe to such a degree that their migrations into Europe can no longer be stopped. The clashes between them and the ruling European nations has become evident with the increased violence. Rapes and murders by Muslims have become epidemic. In Africa, Christians were beheaded and enslaved by the Muslims.

72f. Sixth Seal: This seal is marked by a great earthquake such as the world has never seen and the sun turning to blackness (an unpredicted eclipse?). The moon turns to blood and thus does not appear to be involved in the eclipse, indicating another planet as the source of the eclipse. Stars fall from the skies as rain (meteor shower that hits earth directly). Every geological feature of the earth is shaken and mountains are removed and added elsewhere. This kind of event has not been seen since the time of Moses when the Red Sea was parted. Descriptions of events like these took place all over the world at the time of the Red Sea. In America, they were placing bets where the sun would rise and they recorded that mountains suddenly appeared where there were none before (*Papal Vul*). Cities will fall due to the destruction that takes place during this time. The resulting chaos will allow a *new government to form*. The Anti-Christ will rise up to take his final ruling place over the world and the entire world will see him as some kind of savior.

73. Revelations 7: Silence before the seventh seal: Four angels are holding back the winds from the earth. No winds are allowed to flow for a short time. This could be because the events from the 6ᵗʰ seal from the effects of the cosmic interference causes the earth to temporarily stop moving in the solar system. Here we see the 144,000 from sealed from the 12 tribes. These 144,000 are not sealed until this moment. Any denomination believing that they are part of this 144000 from before this time (2031 A.D.) has not fully understood Revelations. This sealing takes place now and not before. Then John sees the multitudes who gave their lives up for HaShem during the Great Tribulation.

74. Revelations 8: Seventh Seal: Great Tribulation: The silence lasted about a half an hour. Yeshua opens the seal *still in heaven*. Seven angels are given seven trumpets. The censer was filled with fire from the altar and another huge earthquake takes place unlike any before it.

    74a. First Trumpet: Hail and fire mixed with blood fell to the earth. One third of the vegetation on earth is destroyed. This fire causes earth wide forest fires. There is no telling from the text how long these forest fires burn, but they destroy a third of the forests and jungles.

    74b. Second Trumpet: A great mountain of land (asteroid?) fell into the sea causing a third of the sea to turn to blood. A third of the sea creatures and ships were destroyed by this mountain of land. It is likely that this takes place while the forest fires are still burning around the globe. While the narrative gives the trumpets in order, there is no way of knowing if the trumpets followed closely upon one another and took place during the same time frame.

    74c. Third Trumpet: The star called *wormwood* falls and poisons one third of the fresh waters on earth. Many men died from the poisoned waters. It is unlikely that since the fresh waters are scattered around the world, for a single star to have an effect on all of them. This poison is likely from radioactivity. This could be the nuclear fallout from a nuclear bomb that is so large it resembled a star. This radioactivity does not seem to *directly* affect men, but rather causes the waters to be radioactive and made poisonous.

    74d. Fourth Trumpet: The great lights of the skies, sun and moon, are darkened for a third of the day. This would imply a great planet that is close to earth and blocks the lights of the sun, moon, and stars. It could also imply a huge overcast of smoke and clouds such that the lights are shut out, but only a third.

The first three trumpets would only have an effect on non-believers. It is the belief here that HaShem will provide for true believers during these days. The fourth trumpet will have an effect on everyone on earth. The darkness for one third of the day will be for everyone.

74e. Angels of Woe: These angels forecast the woes that follow from the next three angels.

75. Revelations 9-11: Seventh Seal Continued: This seal is opened after the announcement of the angel for the next three angels.

75a. Fifth Trumpet: First Woe: The star that falls must be a fallen angel that has the key to the bottomless pit. The smoke was huge, very likely visible around the globe, as it cut off sunlight. The locusts are not normal locusts that eat grasses and grains, but rather demonic locusts sent to attack any human without the seal of HaShem. This tells us that there are many on earth who are believers still and have not been resurrected. Those without the mark of HaShem will be tormented by the locusts for 5 months. This alone should tell us that the scroll of the seven seals is not just a 7 year period, but of a much longer period. The tormented will seek death and will not find it. The locusts had a king which is significant to tell us that these were demonized locusts, not just biological insects.

75b. Sixth Trumpet: Second Woe: After the 5 months, four angels are told to let loose to slay one third of the men (again, those without the mark of HaShem). They are loosed to deal their death for 1 year, 1 month, 1 day, and 1 hour. This is 9385 hours by the 360 day per year standard. The number of horsemen was 200,000,000. Yet even after seeing so many die, those living without the seal of HaShem refuse to repent.

75c. **Angel of 7 thunders:** John was not allowed to reveal the words of the angel of the 7 thunders. John is forced to eat the little book. He is told that he will prophesy to many peoples and nations.

75d. Two Witnesses: The inner temple was measured, but the outer was not, as it was given to the gentiles for 42 months. This is equivalent to 3 and ½ years. The two witnesses will prophesy during this time for 1,260 days. In a 360 day year, this is exactly 3 and a half years. It is the belief in this revised version that some cosmic interference in the earth's motion around the sun will restore the original 360 day revolution, from our known 365.2422 days of revolution. There will be no rain for the entire duration of their time. If anyone tries to hurt them, they will spew fire and kill anyone trying to hurt them, during this time. At the end of their time, the beast from the bottomless pit will kill them. The people of the earth will rejoice over their deaths for 3 days.

It would appear that the time of the witnesses starts during the first year of the 7th seal. This is a slight step backward in time but important to keep things relevant The 7 vials have not been opened, and the 7th trumpet has not been sounded.

Interestingly, the City of Jerusalem is referred to here as Sodom and Egypt, but is the same city where Yeshua was crucified, so it is talking about Jerusalem. It is an implication here that Jerusalem no longer belongs to the Jews at this crucial point.

At the end of the 3 days, the two witnesses come back to life, horrifying the people of the earth. Then they are taken up to heaven. In that same hour, a great earthquake hits that destroys part of the city as well as many cities around the world. Seven thousand men are killed in the city of Jerusalem alone. This ends the second woe. With the expansion of the internet throughout the world, everyone will be able to witness this as predicted.

76. Revelations 11:15 - 12: Seventh Trumpet: Third Woe: The statement that is made is that the nations of the world have become the kingdoms of our Lord. This means that the yovel contract has been made complete. Yeshua, our kinsman, has successfully taken back the deed to the earth and Satan has lost the power to rule over the earth. *This is the Genesis connection*. The Ark of the Testament (of Moses) is in heaven. They Yovel feast has been satisfied. This year and the next year will be the years of the Yovel (year 49 and year 50 or Year 5999 and Year 6000).

76a. Woman with Child: Great care has to be taken here about interpreting the meaning of the woman and the dragon. We are given a big hint about the dragon in that he took a third of the stars with him. This is what Lucifer did when he rebelled against HaShem with his impossible thought. The child is taken up to HaShem and His Throne, which suggests that the Child is the Savior. The woman must hide for 3 and a half years (but this takes place after Lucifer is cast out of heaven). The battle between Michael and Lucifer starts at the beginning of year 1 of the 7ᵗʰ Seal or year 1 of the week of Tribulation.

The dragon, Lucifer, is cast down and is never allowed back into heaven again. This takes place exactly 3 and half years into the final week of the Yovel which is the Tribulation. A great declaration takes place and Lucifer is no longer allowed to accuse the saints as he was able during the time of Job. At this time, Lucifer in his anger, seeks the woman, but she is hid for the last 3 and half years of the Tribulation.

It is the belief of this revised interpretation that the *true believers in Christ* are represented by the woman and true believers will need to hide and remain hidden until the time of the rapture for the last 3 and a half years.

77. Revelation 13: The Final Beast: The beast is related to the beasts and the image of Nebuchadnezzar and Daniel. The 10 heads represent the final 10 nations, of which one of them will rise above the other. The beasts were all beasts from Daniel's vision, so that this beast is the conglomeration of all the previous empires that have come before. The head that died and rose again became the worshipped false savior of the people. Here is where this author does not believe that the resurrection has taken place yet, in that the beast was given power to war *against the saints*. According to those who believe in a pre-tribulation rapture, all the saints are in heaven. This states explicitly that this is not true. Their explanation is that these are saints that became believers after the rapture, but not once in John has he mentioned a rapture or rising of the dead and this would imply *another resurrection has to take place*. The second beast has the power to do miracles and make believers in the world of the first beast. It is he who institutes the mark of the beast so that any who do not have the mark cannot buy or sell at the market place. This tends to lead to the conclusion that many saints are still living within the cities of the non-believers. This part of the vision seems to go back in time a little ways, to before the seventh seal is opened, which first mentioned the 144,000.

78. Revelation 14: Sealed: This is the first mention of the Lamb on Mount Sion, standing with the 144,000 who were pure. This is the first time that an angel is allowed to preach a gospel, the *Everlasting Gospel*. Within the New Testament, angels were not allowed to preach the gospel, but had to send people to someone who could preach the gospel to them. Now the angel is allowed to preach this last gospel.

Another angel announces the final fall of Babylon (which was the first Empire and has retained some power since it first existed through all the other empires created by Cush/Nimrod). The Babylon Empire first appeared in Genesis, another connection between Genesis and Revelation. The angels with the sickles are the first sign that HaShem's followers are taken up. This is the first true mention of rapture in the Revelation of John. This takes place during the last 3 and a half years of the tribulation, at the end of the week.

79. Revelation 15: Sea of Glass: The Sea of glass which was empty earlier in Revelation is now full of the saints that persevered, martyrs. They will sing before HaShem throughout eternity.

80. Revelation 16: Seven Plagues: It is the belief here that before the plagues are given, the saints have indeed been taken up so that they do not suffer the plagues. This is why the date of the rapture is never known for sure. It happens anytime from the time that the Dragon is cast down from earth (during year 3-4 of the Tribulation Week) until the sealing of the saints.

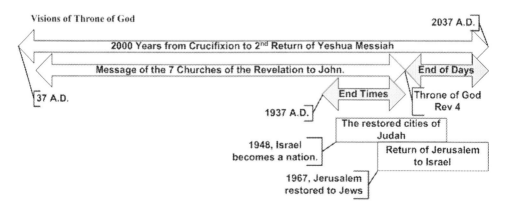

80a. First Vial: The first vial is sores that falls upon all men *who worship the image (of the beast)*. There is still some sign that believers have not yet been taken up, yet the following plagues do not support this.

80b. Second Vial: The entire sea became as blood. Everything in the sea dies. This is a reverse of the creation week.

80c. Third Vial: The rivers and lakes of the land waters became blood as well, killing all that lived with them.

80d. Fourth Vial: The earth was scorched with great heat to scorch men's bodies, but in spite of this, men / women did not repent but cursed HaShem. This to this author seems amazing. They *knew* the source of their suffering and yet refused to bow their knees to Him.

80e. Fifth Vial: Darkness covered the earth. The scorching had caused severe sores and pain. They gnashed their teeth.

80f. Sixth Vial: the River, Euphrates, is dried up that divides the East from the West, allowing the East to prepare to attack the west. While these events seem to be and are supernatural, the events of our political present are still taking place. The Chinese and the Russians band together to make an attack against the West. The spirits (frogs) go out to gather the armies. After this is the mention of the Yeshua coming as a thief in the night. This was mentioned in paragraph 75. No one knows the day and hour of His return. This Return (Rapture) takes place any time during the seven plagues according to the way this is phrased.

80g. Seventh Vial: The great voice comes from the Temple declaring that it is done. The seven seals that bound the deed to earth have been undone by the Lamb of God and the earth is taken back by God from Satan by the kinsman of man, Yeshua. This happens before the final battle at Armageddon. The question remains is that if the saints have been taken up to heaven, then what is this battle all about? Who are the good guys remaining on Earth to participate in this battle?

A great earthquake affecting the entire earth takes place and major cities are destroyed. Land forms are displaced. Jerusalem is divided into 3 parts. Babylon is destroyed. Great hail stones fall upon men, killing many of them. This is the last plague, of hail.

81. Revelations 17: Babylon the Whore: The religious whore of Babylon sits on a beast with 10 horns and seven heads. This vision could have started anytime during the seven seals. The beast *was, is not, and shall rise again out of the bottomless pit.* It is the belief here that this represents a particular person, while the heads and horns represents kingdoms who follow the beast throughout history. This man of perdition is referring to Judas Iscariot who was called the *Son of Perdition. He was*, meaning, he lived at one time, and *then was not*, which means he died (hung himself and then went to perdition), and *then will rise again* out of perdition. The seven heads are seven hills (Rome), which has been the dark side of Christianity since the beginning of the Bishop of Rome as the head of the church, who later was made into a pope. The Supreme Pontiff is the original title of Nimrod as the head of the Tower of Babel Temple to Jupiter is the same title as used by the Pope. This signifies that the modern world is still ruled by the Babylonian Empire of Nimrod and Cush.

This again ties Genesis directly to Revelation, in one swoop. Of the kings, 5 are fallen (Cain, Egypt, Babylon, Persia, Greece), *one is*, meaning that one kingdom is still ruling the world *at the time of John's writing* (Rome), and *one is not yet come (in John's time)*, the Empire at the end of the 6000 years. The final rule of the Anti-Christ is the 8th King that is not shown in the horns but told to us by the angel. The son of perdition was *of the 7 (meaning he was part of the 5 + Rome + the last empire)*. The ten horns are ten kings who have power a single hour with the beast. The ten kings will be a mixture of Christian kings and Muslim kings who have come to some kind of truce (refer to Daniel's image of the ten toes from the dream of Nebuchadnezzar). At this point, using the term Christian is deceiving as these Christian rulers are anything but followers or true believers in HaShem. They are the remnant of blasphemers.

They shall rule for one hour: One week = 7 years.
One day = 1 year = 360 days
One hour = 15 days

The time of this rule is sometime within the last Yovel, but again, it would appear that this particular part of John's vision is not in chronological order with the previous chapters, but goes back in time to the beginning of the Yovel at some point. It is believed here that the rise of the Son of Perdition, Judas, happens during the opening of either seal 1 or seal 2, by the Lamb of God.

At the time of this writing, the Muslim Religion has gained considerable power in Europe and the struggle for dominance as a religion over the Jews and the Christians has started. Atheists and non-believers have somehow taken up sides with the Muslims against the Christians, which results in a huge number of martyrs during the 7 years of the 5th seal.

The original Babylon was one of the empire cities of Nimrod, the son of Cush, the son of Ham. In archaeology, the city of Babylon was called Kish, or Cush (spellings are only different due to the modern historian interpretations of the language before they had a key to understand the ancient languages), named after the son of Ham, who was the original builder of the city of Babylon (a name applied to the city later under Moses).

Babylon is the first known empire of the world and while the Bible indicates that Nimrod was the ruler, his father Cush is listed in archaeological records as the first king. Cush was also listed among the first kings of China, India, and Ethiopia.

More importantly, Babylon, as an empire, became the first religion that went against the religion of Cush's grandfather, Noah. It was the first religion that introduced multiple gods, the leading one being Marduk (Jupiter) at the Temple of the Tower of Babel. The tower was a tower meant to draw the people into one unity against HaShem and also a temple to worship celestial "gods". Thus it became the Whore of the World, or the first false religion. That "whore" culminates into the LAST known false religion of the world in the Last Days. The tower of Babylon was actually a carryover from before the Flood of Noah. The Tower of Babel is believed to have been built on the Temple of Eridu, built by Irad, the grandson of Cain early in the history of the world.

82. Revelations 18: Revelation 18 does follow Revelation 17 in chronological order in showing the results of the 7 kingdoms. Merchants (i.e. the elite and rich among the nations) have become abundant. This is evident by our current society which is divided by class based on financial wealth. The destruction of Babylon will take place in 1 day. Everywhere, people will see the destruction of Babylon (which is located in Iraq). It has been interpreted for many years that Babylon represented the false Christian Church, but Babylon is a Muslim city, and a wealthy one at that.

The oil of the Arabs have made many around the world rich. Nevertheless, Babylon will fall in one day and no one will buy from the city again. It is from the Muslims that the Christians (all Christians, both true and false) have become considered as criminals and abusers of humanity.

83. Revelations 19-20: Marriage of the Lamb and Last Battle: The lamb is called the Word of God. In the gospel of John, John refers to Yeshua as the Word of God *who was at the beginning.* It was the Word of God that was part of the creation process in Genesis. This is one of the most important connections between Genesis and Revelation in that Yeshua was there at the beginning and He is there at the end! The creation week started the Yovel count which ends with Yeshua in this Revelation.

The actual marriage of the church (spiritual church, not any one denomination or physical entity) takes place. When Yeshua rose the first time, from the grave, he took with him all those who had died *before but believed.* This would include all the Old Testament prophets and believers. They were dead and He unlocked their graves and took them to heaven with Him. These are *not* the members of the bride. These are the wedding *guests.* They have been in heaven now along with the Groom for almost 2000 years waiting for the bride to show up. This pattern is the only pattern given for our traditional weddings that is given in the Bible. Our western wedding ceremony cannot be found in the Bible, but was described in the Book of Prayer from the Anglican Church of England. Revelations 19 says that *only now, is the marriage of the Lamb come.* The seals have been broken, but still Yeshua is not yet descended into earth. He is still in heaven at this moment. Blessed is anyone called to be part of the marriage. They are the true believers.

The battle that followed defeated the beast and the false prophet and put them into the Lake of the Fire. The vultures and birds of prey would feast on the dead. The armies of the beast gathered together against Yeshua. An angel takes hold of the dragon, Lucifer or Satan, and binds him for 1000 years. This 1000 years *follows all the events of Revelation and is the 7ᵗʰ day of creation by figurative language or the Millennium of Peace.*

Yeshua Messiah rules for 1000 years along with all those who died for Him or received His mark. The rest of the dead remained in the grave.

This fulfills Yeshua's role as *King of Kings*, which before now had not been fulfilled. Early in the gospels, Yeshua says that His Kingdom has not yet come.

This is the *first resurrection* where the saints are taken up. This is followed by 1000 years of Yeshua's rule, represented by day 7 of the Creation Week. It is a day (1000 year day) of rest.

83a. Satan loosed: After a 1000 years, Satan is loosed again and roams the earth gathering his army. Many *end time interpreters* have tried to place Magog and Gog. What they don't understand is that our current division of nations is not necessarily the same as after a 1000 years have passed. The amazing thing is that this implies that even after a 1000 years of having no Satan to deceive us, in the end, many will still be deceived on earth and become part of Satan's army.

83b. Judgment Day: Following this final battle when the deceived and Satan are cast into the Lake of Fire for all eternity, every man and woman will stand before HaShem with the Books of Life open. Any person that has ever lived will be judged by this book and those not found in it will also be cast into the lake of the fire. This is the *second death*. This death is eternal.

84. Revelations 21: New universe: The earth and the universe are destroyed as they are witnesses of the sins of men and since there should be no remembrance of sin for the *living who survived the second death,* the witnesses have to be removed. A *new heaven and earth* is created.

84a. Bride of HaShem: This is the New Jerusalem, prepared as a bride for HaShem. Yeshua's bride was the church, but Jerusalem, the Holy City is the bride of the Most High. There was no Temple this time as the Most High and the Lamb *are the temple.* There is no mention of the Shekinah Glory or that which is referred to by Christians as the *Holy Spirit.*

85. Revelations 22: Tree of Life: A river flowed out of the throne of God and the Tree of Life. Each month the tree bore a different fruit. We cannot limit ourselves to believe that this is a 12 month cycle as time will change. There will be no night, which means that the solar system will not function as it does now. The earth will not rotate or revolve around a sun. The Lord will supply the light for the earth.

CHAPTER 11

PLAN OF HASHEM

86. The Plan of HaShem: This plan has lightly been touched upon in previous chapters. Within the history of the church, the leaders of the church have implied that HaShem is mysterious and only those within the inner circle of religious leaders know how to decipher that mystery. This work proposes that HaShem is a God of full disclosure. Right from the first chapter of Genesis, HaShem revealed His overall plan for mankind. The 7 days representing 7000 years of mankind's history/future. Again, in Genesis, Isaac, the son of Abraham predicts with amazing accuracy the coming of Yeshua, the Son of HaShem.

87. Moses: In covering "types" it has been revealed that Isaac was a strong type of Yeshua Messiah. Moses on the other hand, while considered by some to be another type of Messiah, is actually a type of HaShem's plan for the world. His life can be divided into 3 periods of 40 years each. In our interpretation, each of those 40 years represents 2000 year periods, or 40 * 50 (the number of years in a Yovel period). This ties Moses strongly to our Yovel.

In the first 40 years of Moses, he was basically an Egyptian without knowledge of HaShem or at least without a strong knowledge. This goes along with what Paul calls the Age of Ignorance or the first 2000 years of history before Abraham appears on the scene.

After Moses murders an Egyptian, he flees to the area now referred to as Saudi Arabia, where his future family lives. Zipporah, his wife, is a daughter of a man who worships HaShem. There Moses leaves a humble life as one of the shepherds for his 2nd 40 years. By definition, he becomes a Jewish Patriarch for 40 years, and is the last patriarch of the Period of Patriarchs, started by Abraham. This 40 years refers to the Time of the Jews, or 2008 A.T. to the crucifixion of Yeshua in 4000 A.T. (37 A.D.)

Time of the Jews: 2008 A.T. to 4000 A.T.

75	430 Patriarchs	430 Judges	430 Kings	75	70	483	Times of Believers (1993 Years)	7	Kingdom Age (1000 Years)
	1290 years of Daniels vision					Daniel's 490 years (483 + 7)	Dispersal of the Jews	7	
	1440 Years					553			
	1440 + 553 + 7 = 2000 years of the Times of the Jews								
						Times of the Gentiles			
Egyptian Old Kingdom	Egyptian Hyksos Period	Egyptian New Kingdom							
	Arabic Nations of Ishmael								

Then Moses is tending the sheep when he turns to see a strange sight. He sees a bush burning, but not being consumed by the flames. Then he hears the actual voice of HaShem calling to him. Ordering him to return to Egypt to free the Hebrew slaves. This starts the last 40 years of Moses where he is the first judge of Israel leading into the Period of the Judges. Samuel was the last judge of this period, also serving 40 years as a judge. This period refers to the last 2000 years where the people are no longer led by religious leaders (patriarchs and judges) but rather by the Shekinah Glory, referred to by modern churches as the Holy Spirit on an individual level.

This is a total of 120 Yovels, or 120 years of Moses' life. It has already been mentioned that Revelations is the prediction of the entire 3rd period of Moses' life, with the 7 churches and the prediction of the End of Days and the Wrath of HaShem.

88. HaShem's Wrath: Throughout the history of mankind, we can see evidence of HaShem's judgment and His wrath. I can remember in my High School Humanities class, my teacher (an anti-God believer) made the point that in the Old Testament, HaShem was a God of wrath but changed to a God of mercy after the Crucifixion. I wasn't a strong believer then and had almost no knowledge of HaShem, but even then, I wondered about a God just changing like that. That didn't make sense. God (as I knew Him then) was still a God and unchangeable. Now more than ever, I believe I have proven that to be true. HaShem is a God of BOTH judgement and mercy and has been throughout the entire history of mankind.

The rules were given to Moses, (although there is strong evidence that patriarch's before Moses knew of those rules before the Tablets of Moses were given). If we break the rules, we suffer the consequences. Here's the catch. Only on person in history has ever been able to keep all the rules without ever breaking a single one; Yeshua Messiah. This doesn't appear to give the rest of mankind much hope from Hashem's wrath. And in truth, everyone from the dawn of time, save Yeshua, deserves HaShem's wrath.

Added to this, Lucifer (Satan, The Deceiver) constantly accuses us and demands justice from HaShem against mankind.

89. HaShem's Mercy: There is one saving grace. True, we each deserve HaShem's wrath, no matter how innocent you might believe you are, but we can rely on the MERCY of HaShem. His mercy was given to us through Yeshua on the Cross.

90. Lucifer's defeat: When Adam and Eve sinned, they basically sold the deed to the Earth to Lucifer. This is the scroll that is in heaven and sealed by the seven seals which only the innocent Lamb of HaShem is able to open. Lucifer's deception was intended to lead mankind to destruction, but Lucifer had a plan.

If he could get mankind to sin, Lucifer knew that God's justice would demand that HaShem punish mankind with the same judgment given to Lucifer and the fallen ones. And Lucifer knew that HaShem loved mankind far more than the fallen angels who had turned away from HaShem. HaShem would be in conflict as to what to do. If HaShem forgave mankind of their sin, then HaShem's justice would demand that HaShem also forgive the fallen angels, including Lucifer. This was Lucifer's ultimate plan in the Garden. The deception of Eve was far more devious than just an obvious breaking of the rules. If Lucifer could be forgiven, he would be given another chance to overthrow the Throne of HaShem.

Lucifer didn't understand at that time the significance of Hashem's plan. This is the most important part of HaShem's plan in the history of mankind and we can see it over and over throughout the Bible. HaShem did condemn Adam and Eve and therefore all mankind for their sin. They were cast out of Eden. But then HaShem did something amazing. He paid the price of our sin FOR US on the Cross. His only begotten Son sacrificed for our sins as the Laws of Moses demanded for the price of sin. And many who don't understand this ask: What kind of God sacrifices His own son, especially an innocent son guilty of no sin? Again, we underestimate HaShem. Yeshua Messiah was raised from death on the 3rd day. At that moment, Lucifer understood his defeat.

91. The Plan of HaShem: HaShem's plan is so many levels deep. It concerns the salvation of mankind at the highest level and yet consists of so many levels below that as well, as throughout history we are able to see how He knew what would happen. From the murder of the Egyptian by Moses, to the Red Sea. From the birth of Isaac to the Birth of Yeshua at the human level. On Day 1, HaShem knew each of us and every thought and action we would take in our time. He knew how many hairs we would have on our head at any given moment. He knew how we would fail, but gave us a way out. If we believe on He who hung on the cross, we can be released from the judgment of HaShem at the end of the 7000 years of mankind on Judgment Day.

Printed in the United States
By Bookmasters